THE
ASHES
OF A
GOD

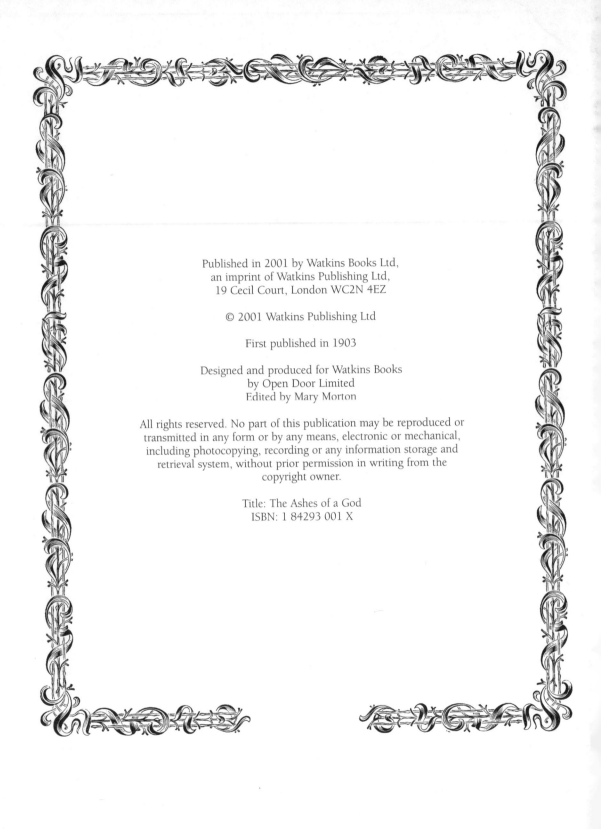

Published in 2001 by Watkins Books Ltd,
an imprint of Watkins Publishing Ltd,
19 Cecil Court, London WC2N 4EZ

© 2001 Watkins Publishing Ltd

First published in 1903

Designed and produced for Watkins Books
by Open Door Limited
Edited by Mary Morton

Title: The Ashes of a God
ISBN: 1 84293 001 X

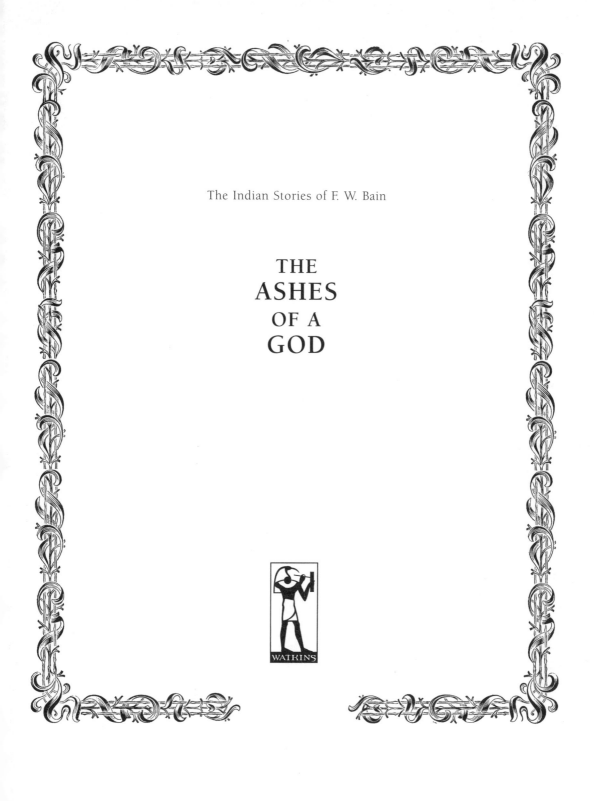

The Indian Stories of F. W. Bain

THE
ASHES
OF A
GOD

Dedicated to one that is taken
and two that are left

Ah! wouldst thou then redream the love of yore?
Bind on thy heart the wings of Memory,
And hie thee to an unforgotten shore
Across the sea.

Oh hie thee to the land, where, constant still,
While golden distance hid the years to be,
We watched the suns go down behind the hill
Across the sea.

Now has our own Affection sunk to rest;
Set is the Sun of love for thee and me,
And rows of Clouds weep in the wild red West
Across the sea.

Bhárgawa

CONTENTS

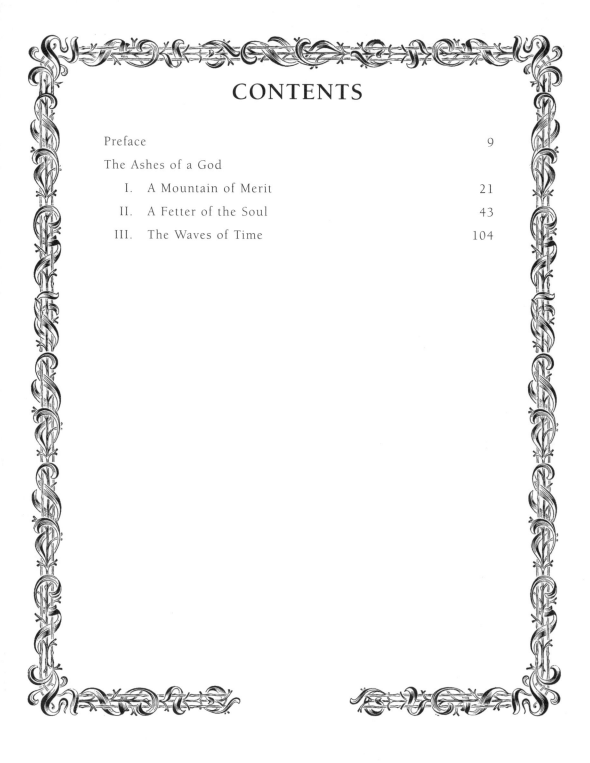

Preface   9

The Ashes of a God

I.   A Mountain of Merit   21

II.   A Fetter of the Soul   43

III.   The Waves of Time   104

PREFACE

HAT mischief-making deity, the god of Love, who delights in getting others into trouble, got himself, once upon a time, if we may trust the poets, into trouble of no ordinary kind. For seeing, as he thought, his opportunity, he attempted to inflame Maheshwara himself with passion for the virgin Daughter of the Snow, who was standing shyly just in front of him, like an incarnation of irresistible seduction, raised to the highest power by the contrast between her coarse bark garments and the perfect beauty of the figure they enclosed. And then it was that the biter was bit, and Love himself was suddenly reduced to ashes for his impudence by a pulverising glance from the angry Maheshwara's terrible third eye, that opened for an instant, for unhappy Love's discomfiture, like the door of a blast-furnace upon a moth. And the pale young Moon looked out upon it all, from the hair of the angry god; the pale new Moon, that very Digit, who gives the title to our story, being therein described as so superlatively lovely, as to be 'capable of causing the very god of Love to rise from his own ashes.'

For it is to be remembered that Love's ashes are no common ashes: they have in them something of the phoenix; they are always ready to revive. The beautiful lament of Rati – Love's wife –, over the ashes of her husband – overheard by Kálidás –, was really, had she only known, superfluous. He was sure to come to life again. Or, to speak plain English, a great passion is immortal: its very ashes are never absolutely dead. Breathe close upon them, and, as one of our own poets has said, it may be flame will leap. And this is the solid reason why the old Hindoo sages denoted both Love and Recollection by one and the same word. Memory, remembrance, regret, reminiscence; – all these are clearly closely akin, near relatives of Love. What is indifferent to us we soon forget; but we remember what we love, and the longer, in proportion as we love it more. And thus it comes about, that the most formidable obstacle to the would-be sage, the candidate for honours, as we might call him, in renunciation of the world, is his own recollection, his memory of the past.

The object of the sage, according to the old Hindoo doctrine, is to become absolute master of himself – 'jitátmá' –, to render himself completely superior, or rather indifferent, to the 'attachment' of all mundane clogs. The ordinary mortal is a prisoner, tied, bound in bondage, or 'attached' – 'sakta' –, to and by the objects of delusion and sense. Whoever aims at emancipation must first, by a long and strenuous course of penance and austerity, sever these attachments, till even though he still remains among them, they run off him like water from a duck; and he goes on living, according to the classic formula, like a wheel that continues to revolve when the original impetus has ceased, or like a branch that goes on swaying after the departure of the bird. He is 'awake,' as opposed to those who still remain blinded by illusion; he is 'free,' as contrasted with the bound; his soul is unattached. But now, there is one thing, from which it may very well be doubted, whether even any sage, no matter what his elevation, was ever wholly free – regret. The strongest soul possesses the most powerful recollection, and unless madness intervene, to cut the thread by obliterating memory, there are things that refuse to be forgotten. And where recollection is, there is sure to be were it but a vestige of regret; for memory is love. And what, then, is it, that is of all things most peculiarly the object of regret; that laughs at all efforts to reduce it to oblivion and nonentity; that refuses to be driven into the oubliettes of any soul? Needless to say, a woman. And therefore it is, that she is regarded, in Oriental mysticism, as beyond all other things the enemy of emancipation; the clog par excellence; the fetter of the soul; the everlastingly regretted, the unforgettable and unforgotten; the irreducible residuum; the inextinguishable spark among the ashes of the past. Was it not Swift, among whose papers, after his death, was found a packet, labelled in his own handwriting: 'Only a woman's hair'? And did not Coriolanus find in this the thing to thwart him, the obstacle that stood between his resolution and the overthrow of Rome? But we need not go to history or fiction to prove a thing endorsed by the experience of almost every man and woman since the beginning of the world. Everybody knows, what one has said, that youth is a blunder: manhood a struggle: old age a regret. Death is preceded by a sigh; did ever anybody die, who had absolutely nothing to regret? And regret, in the language of the old Hindoos, is nothing but the ashes of dead love, not utterly extinct; and therefore, since all love is more or less divine, 'the ashes of a god.'

The ethical value of India's beautiful mythology is not sufficiently appreciated in Europe, whose people seem to think that virtue was discovered by themselves, and have learned from Xenophanes and Plato, S. Paul, S. Augustine, and other shallow politicians to deny all morality to polytheism,[1] condemning the whole of antiquity for the vices of the old metropolis of Rome, which itself was no worse than many modern cities. And India is a survival from antiquity. But it is not, as some suppose, a sink of immorality; nor a barbarous 'tabula rasa,' as others seem to think, with everything to learn in ethics, on which anything may be written that you please. The arrogance of ignorance is the cause of these misunder-standings. The Hindoos have a fable that the 'chakora,' a legendary partridge, subsists on the beams of the moon: and the bird is no bad emblem of themselves. In the ruin of all their ancient glories, the one thing that remains to them is the thesaurus of religion and mythology preserved, like palaeozoic flies in amber, in the crystal of their ancient tongue, whose presiding genius is the moon. For with them it is not as with us. Here, in the young nations of the West, literature and religion are not one thing, but two, with essences and origins altogether different and distinct, though now

[1] *The old argument: there is immorality in the stories of the gods; ergo, the men must be the same, is a monotheist calumny. Books like Kingsley's 'Roman and Teuton,' where all the vice is imputed to the Roman, and all the virtue to the Teuton, are merely an inversion of the fact. 'The truth is,' says Professor Lewis Campbell on Aeschylus, 'that while religious custom lay upon the Greeks with a weight almost as deep as life, the changing clouds of mythology rested lightly on their minds, and were in their very nature, to some extent, the sport of fancy and imagination.' This is equally true of the Hindoos.*

and then, a Milton or a Dante may, by welding them together, produce something more analogous to Indian poetry. For in India religion and literature are inseparable: they look back not to Greece on the one hand and Judaea on the other, but to a sacred compound of the two, all the nearer because it is their very own, whereas to us both Greece and Judaea are foreign, not only the places but the tongues, and likely in the immediate future to become still stranger than they are. This is why nobody can possibly understand anything of India who is ignorant of Sanskrit, which is the key to India, and from which all the modern local idioms, be they Aryan or not, borrow almost everything literary, religious, or philosophical that they contain.[1] And this is just where all the missionaries stumble. Few or none of them realise what it is they have against them: an obstacle which even Ganesha could hardly overcome. You must obliterate the languages of India, ancient and modern, before you can alter its religion. It will not be easy, for when you have succeeded in consigning to oblivion both Sanskrit and Pálí, which seems every day less probable, you will still have to reckon with the vernaculars, with Tulsi Das and Tukarám, Kabir, and a score of other Bibles of the Hindoo peoples, not to mention the legion of their legends, stories, proverbs, festivals, and songs. Fed, like his own 'chakora,' upon these, the Hindoo of good caste finds it impossible to reconcile his traditional conception of saintliness, always ascetic, and based on renunciation, with the spectacle of comfortable missionaries, admirably housed, riding

[1] *The dictum of Mr. Rudyard Kipling, whose India is merely a misrepresented Anglo-India, that 'there ain't no Ten Commandments' there, is superficially a truism, and essentially a foolish libel. No man has done more to caricature and misinterpret India, in the interests of military vulgarity, than this popular writer, to whom Hindoo India is a book with seven seals.*

good horses and possessing coquettish wives whose ample wardrobes savour not of sanctity but of Paris. Buddha, the missionary par excellence, was no low-caste man, making a living out of his profession, but an aristocrat who turned his back upon the world; and a dozen English dukes or earls coming out to India to practise voluntary asceticism would do more to convince the Hindoos of Christian religion and sincerity than any number of missionary conferences, in which the real obstacle to missionary effort, the fact, well known to the Hindoo, that he is invited to accede to a religion abandoned by the intelligence of Europe, is scrupulously hidden out of sight. From every line of his old literature the Hindoo learns the essence of religion better than any missionary can teach him. It is devotion: of a woman, to her husband; of a man, to his duty, his 'dharma'; his ancestors, his family, his mother-tongue. Nothing ever will persuade a sane Hindoo of reputable family to belong to a religion which bids him, by injunction, sanction, or example, to abandon his ancestors, desert his family, eat beef, drink spirits, and apply to the divorce court. So it is that we see in India at the present day the very same phenomenon that was exhibited in the agony of the ancient world, when Christianity was an asylum for the outcaste and the criminal and the pariah, a refuge for the destitute, like Romulean Rome in Livy's legend.

This old Sanskrit language, then, in which dwells the spirit of a classic paganism not less beautiful, and holier than Hellas, pre-

Christian, idolatrous,[1] preserves among other things opposed to Western modernism an element of charm, which in Europe too much knowledge is destroying: the element of distance, of the unknown, of that which is outside the map, beyond, afar. For us, the time is gone, when, as Plutarch says, geographers filled up the emptinesses beyond the limits known with bogs or deserts or wild beasts. But Hindoo stories move in an enchanted land, a thing to dream over like 'the world as known to Homer,' or the scraps of mythological geography in Pindar's Odes, when, for example, Rhodes was not an island, but lay lurking, before the gods divided earth, in the briny hollows of the sea,[2] And as we pore on it, we feel ready to murmur with Voltaire, that error has its worth as well as truth. Did the discovery of America make up for the lost mystery that brooded like the spirit over the waters of the dim Atlantic, when even Hibernia was half a myth, 'ultra quam ad occasum nulla invenitur habitabilis terra, nisi miranda loca quae vidit S. Brandanus in Oceano'?[3] The old literature of India, its epics and 'itihases,' are the very home of mythical geography, of lotus lands, white islands, seas of milk, and distant hills behind which, far beyond the sea, the suns go down to die, which never even Sindbad saw. It is all one gigantic dream, fairy tale reduced to a kind of system, where wild imagination is reality, and the commonplace is not. Teach the Hindoo the earth goes round the sun; it may be so: but in his heart there echoes some scrap of ancient poetry, where every sun descends to rest behind the western hill. Would you

---

[1] *The observations of Mr. Theophilus G. Pinches, on the means by which, in ancient Babylon. 'an enlightened monotheism and the grossest polytheism could, and did, exist side by side,' apply accurately to India. – 'The Old Testament in the Light of the Historical Records of Assyria and Babylonia, p. 10.*
[2] *Olymp. vii.*
[3] *'Apud Bocharti Phaleg.' p. 184.*

blame him for choosing rather to err with Kálidás and Walmiki, than go right with some elementary manual of geography? For him, the dream is the reality; and the spell is in the language in which these things are written: who does not know the language cannot understand the spell. Your Mill[1] and your Macaulay argue on these matters like blind men reasoning on colour. Only that grows never old, which never lived. You cannot kill a dream, because it is already dead.

Down in the west of England, on the very edge of the sea, I know a hill, which had it been in India, pagan India, would have been sacred long ago to the Daughter of the Snow; so exactly does its giant sweep of smooth green turf resemble the outline of a colossal woman's breast. And there on a yellow evening, I lay and mused. And I said to my own soul: This is not quite the golden glow of my Indian Eve, for it is just a little chilly; and yet, yonder is a hill worthy to be haunted by Párwati herself. Only the flowers would all be strange to her; for certainly she would not recognise these primroses and buttercups, this gorse. And yet, some things might deceive her; for surely she would take Lundy Island for the very western mountain, behind which at this very moment the sun is going down.

And as I pondered on her and her husband, all at once I exclaimed: O Wearer of the Moony Tire, who art thyself the Past, the Present, and the Future, didst thou for all thy knowledge of

[1] *James Mill's criticism of the Indian ethic is a criminal offence, a sin against literature. The coryphaeus of the Inductive Philosophy, dogmatising on a language of which he could not even read a single word!*

Time's secrets ever dream, that one day thy worshippers would all fall under the direction of this misty little island in a far-off northern sea? Was it irony in the Creator, who makes and ruins even worlds in sport, to subject thy dreaming millions to the Western men of business, less like them than any other people on the surface of the earth? Had India's gods deserted her, as once Judaea's did, or wert thou buried in a thousand years of Yóg, when the Moguls and Maráthas, the Clives and the Dupleix were fighting for the heavy crown glittering with barbaric pearl and gold? And yet, what use in asking, since doubtless thou art far away among thy own Himálaya's still undiscovered snows.

And as I spoke, I looked, and lo! there before me was the almost imperceptible Digit of the Moon, hanging low in the evening sky just over Lundy Island and the sea. And instantly I exclaimed: Aha! Maheshwara, I was wrong, and I utterly forgot thy quality of universal presence, for sure I am that where thy Digit is, thou art thyself not far away. So then tell me, was it thy wish to punish thy devotees, or was it by thy negligence they fell? And what shall be the end?

And as I gazed upon the Moon, I heard the laughter of the deity in the thunder of the waves. And presently he said: Foolish Western, there are many other things thou hast forgotten, as well as my ubiquity. Dost thou not remember what one of thy own philosophers has said: θεὸς ἀναίτιος αἴτια δ' ἑλομἔνου? Or hast thou actually forgotten the wisdom of all my own old Hindoo sages, that thou wouldst saddle the responsibility for the ripening of the fruit of works, on me? As my people's works have been, so is their condition: they are but gathering the fruit of the tree of their own wrong-doing in a previous existence. And the crimes of a former birth dog them like death, and lie on them like a shadow: they only have themselves to blame, and now there is no help for it, but in themselves. And they must work out their own emancipation, not by petulance and violence, but by penance and austerity.

And I listened in silence to the deity, and when he finished, I looked up. And after a while, I said to myself: Now, surely, that crystal moon is the diadem of deity; and the voice of God is the murmur of the sea.

Christmas, 1910

THE ASHES OF A GOD

Where the Snows that fall on the Icy Wall
Leave all the tall peaks bare,
I heard the Mountain Spirits call
that travel upon the air

Chaitya

A MOUNTAIN OF MERIT

INVOCATION

'Sinking in the waves of time, O skull-adorned demolisher of Daksha,[1]
we cling to the worship of the beauty of thy moony tire, whose silver lustre steals like a
woman of good family fearfully through the shadows of the forest of thy hair, to fall at
last like a blue and ashy benediction upon the mountain backs of the three great
worlds, lying prostrate in a "sáshtánga"[2] devotion at thy feet.'

CHAPTER I

FAR away in the northern quarter, half-hidden in Himálaya's shaggy sides, there lies a holy bathing-place and favoured haunt of Hara, where Gangá leaps down through a rocky chasm in the Lord of Hills, and rushes out into the plain, white as it were with foamy laughter at the thought of her coming union with Yamuná and the sea. And there one evening long ago it happened, that two Brahmans were engaged in a dispute upon the bank of that very sacred stream, having quarrelled on a question of precedence. And long they wrangled idly, each claiming a superiority in status which neither would allow. And finally one said: Enough of this absurdity! Who but a blind man argues as to the shining of the sun at noon? Or how can thy family contend in excellence with mine, which is in the 'gotra' of Agastya? Then said the other scornfully: Thou art the proof of

[1] i.e. Maheshwara.
[2] That is, so as to touch the ground 'with all eight parts of the body' at once.

thy own asseveration, and as I think, the very Balákhilyas[1] must have been the original progenitors of such a pigmy as thyself. And the other answered angrily: Better the pigmy body of Agastya than a pigmy soul enclosed in the worthless bulk of such a 'pashu'[2] as thyself. And immediately his opponent ran upon him, and gave him a kick. And he exclaimed: Ha! dost thou call me 'pashu'? then taste my hoof. But as to thy Agastya, a fig for him! What is he to me, who am just about to earn emancipation by a series of extraordinary penances, worthy to extort the admiration of Pashupati[3] himself?

So as those boobies wrangled, it happened, by the decree of destiny, that that very Lord of Creatures animate and inanimate was passing in the air, only just above them, as he roamed towards Kailàs with Gauri in his arms, on his way back from a visit to Ujjayini, one of his earthly homes, whose palaces seem to laugh at their rivals in the sky. And as he listened to the squabble, all at once he uttered a solitary shout of laughter. And instantly, those two very foolish disputants took to their heels, and fled away at full speed in opposite directions, taking his laughter for a thunderbolt. And seeing them go, the Daughter of the Mountain said to her lord: Well might thy laughter be aroused by the exceedingly contemptible behaviour of that pair of silly Brahmans. Then said Maheshwara: Nay, it was not that which caused my laughter. For these ridiculous mortals commonly dispute in precisely this manner, making use of abuse, and even blows, instead of reasoning, blinded by vanity and arrogance and

[1] *Legendary dwarfs. Agastya was a very little man.*
[2] *i.e. an animal, a brute; a synonym for the absence of all culture and intelligence.*
[3] *The Lord of Animals, i.e. Shiwa, is the ascetic par excellence.*

passion. And if I were to laugh at every instance of the kind, I should never stop laughing, night or day. For there is no end to just such arguments as these. Then said Párwati: At what then didst thou laugh? And the moony-crested god said slowly: I laughed, to think of the amazing self-ignorance of that big boasting Brahman. For he is the very man, who in one of his former incarnations so egregiously failed, in exactly such an effort of asceticism as that which he described himself now just about to undergo, though he has utterly forgotten all about it, and never even dreams that he is travelling fast, not towards emancipation, but away from it: since all his acts in recent births are nothing but so many steps downward into the abyss of reincarnation, out of which he will not find it so easy, again to reascend. For when a soul is on the downward path, nothing in the world is so difficult as to alter its direction into that of the ascent, or even to stop at all; seeing that every fresh error adds weight to its burden, and impetus to its speed. And if he only knew it, this down-goer would be utterly appalled at the prospect of the innumerable myriads of years that lie before him, stretching away like a never-ending desert of waterless sand, through which he must absolutely pass, in birth after birth, each terminated by a death, before he will succeed in changing his tendency to darkness. For the waves of the sea of works are over his head, and he resembles a stone, sinking continuously down, down, in a bottomless and clammy slough of evil, created by himself.

Then said Párwati: And what then was this old endeavour, the very recollection of whose contrast with his brag so moved thy laughter? And the god said: It is a long story, and travelling at this pace, if I begin it, we shall arrive at Kailàs long before it ends. But if, as it seems, I must absolutely tell thee all about it, I will regulate the speed of our advance, so as to keep pace with the movement of the tale, ordering matters so, as to arrive at Kailàs and the conclusion of the tale exactly at the same moment. Moreover, it would be a shame to hurry. For I love to watch the lustre of my moon, noiselessly stealing like a thief into the shadowy gorges of thy father's huge valleys, and stripping from his sides that carpet of rich colour which the setting sun bestows upon them, to spread over them instead that cold and melancholy pallor of her own, which resembles an atmosphere of the camphor of death.

CHAPTER II

NOW then, O thou Snowy One, that long ago, in a former birth, this boaster was a Brahman, and his name was Trishodadhi,[1] and he was, by hereditary descent, the minister of a king, named Ruru. And as it happened, King Ruru was a spoiled child. And then, being betrayed by his queen in his youth, he fell into a violent hatred of all women, that, strange to say! exhibited itself in the form of love. For wishing as it were to wreak his vengeance on the whole sex for

---

[1] *i.e. an ocean of thirst. This thirst, 'trishá,' is the technical name for what Schopenhauer calls the 'will to live' – 'vitai semper hiantes.'*

the crime of one, he began like a mad bee to rove furiously from flower to flower, making love to every woman in the world that took his fancy, and then throwing her away as soon as won – taking all possible pains to obtain the love of each, only to flout her, the moment it was his. And like a deadly plague, he gradually corrupted the women of his kingdom, who nearly all found him irresistible, not merely because he was a king, but still more because of his extraordinary beauty, being as he was a good thing changed and converted into evil by the misconduct of his wife. And he was dreaded by the husbands and fathers of his kingdom, and above all by his minister, Trishodadhi. For Trishodadhi possessed a wife much younger than himself, and recently married, named Watsatarí.[1] And she was well named, resembling, in youth and beauty, the horns of the new moon; and she hovered between the charm of the woman and the child, as the moon does between the two incomparable moments of delicate epiphany and round perfection. And yet, unlike the moon, she was always invisible to everybody, save only himself. For his natural jealousy, which was extreme, was accentuated by her extraordinary beauty, and his own age. And fearing all the men in the world, above all he feared the king, and passed his life perpetually trembling lest Ruru should set eyes on her; and he kept her very scrupulously hidden, like a priceless pearl, from all eyes but his own. And though he doted on her, yet against his will he was obliged to leave her much alone, for all the burden of the state was thrown upon his shoulders by the

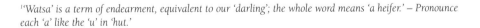
[1]*'Watsa' is a term of endearment, equivalent to our 'darling'; the whole word means 'a heifer.' – Pronounce each 'a' like the 'u' in 'hut.'*

king, who utterly neglected all affairs, intent on nothing but pursuing his amours. And being thus preoccupied, Trishodadhi had only his intervals of leisure for his wife. And yet, all the while he was not near her, he was everlastingly tormented by his jealousy and fear, which like busy painters drew him endless rows of pictures of his wife, surrounded in his absence by innumerable lovers, created out of nothing by his own imagination, and all, as it were, but so many copies of the king; as if, like the slayer of Kamsa,[1] King Ruru possessed the power of self-multiplication, appearing in just as many bodies as he pleased. And though Watsatarí was in reality purer than a tear, he was haunted by a swarm of suspicions, which like bees buzzed for ever in the ear of his uneasy soul, and drove him almost into madness, while like a gardener he strove to preserve his blue honey-laden lotus from the onslaughts of their importunate and greedy troops. And in order to place her as far as possible beyond the reach of any danger, he kept her in a residence that resembled a fortress, and shut her in a garden, surrounded by a lofty wall. And he never went to see her without quivering with anxiety, lest he should discover, on arriving, that what he was always fearing had actually come to pass. And so in fact it did. For one day, returning from his duties long before he was accustomed, as if destiny had determined to gratify his apprehensions, when he entered the garden, where his wife was in the habit of wandering for her diversion, he looked, and saw her, in the very arms of the king.

[1] *i.e. Krishna; who solved Plato's old difficulty of the One and the Many, by 'keeping company' with each of his lovesick milkmaids at once.*

So when he saw it, Trishodadhi stood for a single instant, silent, gazing at that pair with eyes that were suddenly filled to the very brim, first with amazement, and then with anguish, and next with anger, and finally with ice. And then he turned away, saying slowly to himself: Miserable wretches, what after all is the use of astonishment, or pity for myself, or even wrath with you? It is not you that are to blame, obeying as ye do the incorrigible instincts of your sex and your depravity, and rewarding one who has loaded both of you with benefits with the blackness of ingratitude. But it is rather I myself who am to blame, for putting any faith whatever, were it fleeting as a jot of time, in this treacherous and unsubstantial world, filled full to the very brim with lovers and women, snakes and tigers, and betrayers and betrayed; on which I will this very instant turn my back for ever, as indeed, had I not been utterly blinded by passion and delusion, I should have done already, long ago. And even as he said, so he did. And he went straight away, there and then, never to return. And abandoning his wife and his office and his home, counting them all as grass, he threw away his skin, like a snake, and becoming a pilgrim, turned his steps, without losing a single instant, to the wilderness of the Windhya hills.

And as he went along, that very miserable Brahman said angrily to himself, with tears in his eyes: Ha! what was the Creator about, in creating such a world as this, where evil-doers prosper, and virtue comes to ruin, and fidelity and service and devotion gain

nothing in reward, but villainous ingratitude, and bitter disappointment? Surely it was a blunder; and why, then, do the rulers of the world allow it to continue? And all at once, rage rushed into his soul against the very constitution of the world,[1] as if that, rather than himself, were the author of his misery. And he exclaimed, in an ecstasy of grief: Ha! Did not Wishwamitra, when he found this world not according to his tastes, create another of his own? And by what means did he acquire the power that enabled him to perform his extraordinary feats of world-creating and other such miracles, but by penance and asceticism? Did he not prove, by his own example, that nothing is impossible to perfect asceticism? And cannot others do what he did, by the very selfsame means, provided only that their resolution is thorough and complete? So then, now, I also will rival and surpass him, and by means of the intensity of my extraordinary penance bend the very gods to my will, and compel them to obey me, and change the established constitution of the world, whether they will or no. Aye, my resolution is fixed, and adamantine, and inalterable. I will begin this very moment, and heap up for myself a very mountain of merit, till its towering mass shall overbalance and obliterate the united forces of the inhabitants of heaven.

So then he resolved, in the bitter agony of disappointment. And like one looking down into a forest pool created by a shower of rain, and mistaking its shallowness for an infinity of depth, deceived by the imitation of the illimitable abyss of heaven in the

---

[1] 'Sthiti,' the established world-order, is one of the three terms of the universe, as opposed to 'sarga,' its creation, and 'pralaya,' its destruction and end.

mirror of its glass, so he mistook his own pique at the world arising from the wound inflicted by the conduct of his wife, and proving, by its very violence, the strength of his attachment to the objects of sense that he pretended to despise, for real renunciation based on perfect knowledge, and undertook rashly, in imitation of that bull among ascetics, Wishwamitra, a task beyond the limits of his strength; not having understood, that those only are equal to the terrible strain of true renunciation whose soul is pure, unstained by any tincture of egoism, and resembling a well of the crystal liquor of perfect mastery of self. And yet even so, he commenced his undertaking confidently, and counting beforehand on success, and burning with the fire of preliminary zeal, ignorant of the presence of that element in his soul, which was destined in the future to upset his calculations, and bring about his utter destruction, on the very brink of ultimate success. And going to the farthest recesses of the forest, he discovered in its heart a remote and lonely cemetery,[1] on the outskirts of a long deserted and forgotten town. And he entered it, and having discovered a suitable spot, he remained and dwelt there, as motionless as a tree. And collecting from the relics of burning funeral pyres a quantity of bare and empty skulls, divested of their flesh by fire, and time, and the troops of night-walking, flesh-devouring wild beasts and Rákshasas and Wetálas,[2] by which that gloomy cemetery was infested, he made of them a rosary for himself, like mine,[3] and began to mutter spells. And so he continued, night and day, year

29

---

[1] The 'smashána' is rather a burning-ground than a cemetery. But it is often called 'pitrigriha' – 'the home of the fathers,' and thus cemetery may stand, as an equivalent.
[2] i.e. goblins and vampires.
[3] Maheshwara, who is speaking, wears a necklace of skulls.

after year, muttering incessantly, living all the while like a serpent on nothing but air and his own undaunted resolution, till at last he had completed a century of years.

And then at last, being pleased with his perseverance, such as it was, I appeared to him one day in the guise of a 'digambara,'[1] and granted him a boon. Thereupon that indomitable Trishodadhi replied: O Shankara, I ask for absolutely nothing, but permission to continue my devotions. If therefore I must perforce select a boon, grant me as much time as I require, so as to continue, muttering on, till I abandon my assiduity of my own accord. So I left him, muttering diligently away, just as before, though I foresaw the end, and knew that he carried within him, unsuspected by himself, the seed of the fruit of his own undoing, which time would ripen, dooming him to undergo the punishment that lies in wait for all, who plunge, without due consideration, into enterprises above their strength.[2] And so the boon I offered him was wasted, and the chance was thrown away. For had he only had knowledge of himself, it might have saved him after all, by ensuring him oblivion of the past. For his memory was his ruin, as the story will show thee, O Daughter of the Snow.

And he in the meantime muttered on unflaggingly, wholly intent on nothing else, till at length the mound of his accumulated merit began to rival in dimension yonder hill, whose top the evening sun is now touching with the colour of affection, as if loth to leave it to be swallowed by the dark.

[1] *i.e. a naked mendicant ascetic.*
[2] *'Nemo potest supra seipsum,' said the Schoolmen – a profound observation exactly in harmony with old Hindoo ideas on moral force.*

CHAPTER III

ND then at last one day it happened, that Mátali arrived in Indra's palace, having returned to heaven from a visit to the earth. And as soon as he entered, he exclaimed: O punisher of Páka,[1] and the rest, what are you all about? Are you asleep, or have you actually abandoned all care whether of your own pre-eminence or the established order of the world? For away below on earth, there is an old Brahman, in a deserted cemetery in the forest of the Windhya hills, who by his interminable muttering continued through the centuries has accumulated so gigantic a heap of merit,[2] that it threatens destruction to the three worlds. And now, unless something is done very speedily to stop him, and reduce it, this merit of his, beyond a doubt, will disturb the equilibrium of the universe, and wreck the established order of the worlds, and hurl you from your thrones.

And hearing him, Indra said: There is no difficulty in this. I will go myself, and bribe him to discontinue his proceedings. And he went down himself accordingly to earth, to examine and investigate that Brahman, and see what could be done. And after considering him awhile, and admiring his extraordinary obstinacy, he set to work to tempt him, and induce him, by offering bribes of various descriptions, to desist. And he offered him accordingly mountains of gold, and oceans of jewels, and everlasting youth, and many kinds of magic power, and finally he racked his brains, to find

---

[1] *i.e. Indra. Mátali is his messenger, the Hindoo Mercury.*
[2] *This singular idea, familiar now to Europe, in the form of the prayer-wheels of Tibet, is not wholly without parallels in the West. The only difference is, that the Hindoos are a very logical people, and carry the absurd to its extreme.*

something or other that would move that obdurate Trishodadhi, and draw him from his vow. But in vain. For Trishodadhi paid no more attention to his offers and himself, than the moon does to the barking of a dog; continuing to mutter, all the time he spoke, just as if he was not there.

So finding all his efforts vain, after a while, that baffled lover of Ahalyá[1] returned to heaven. And summoning the gods, he laid the case before them, and requested their advice. And after deliberation, they determined to seduce him by sending down a heavenly nymph, saying to themselves: Did not Menaká, and Tilottamá, and others of their kind, prove too strong for the asceticism of even mighty sages, so that their merit melted, like a lump of snow, in the flame of their desire, and their self-control vanished like stubble in a forest conflagration? Nay, did not even Brahma assume his name,[2] becoming four-faced, in order to gratify his intolerable thirst to behold the beauty of Tilottamá performing a 'pradakshina' around him, though he would not turn his head?

Therefore it is not to be doubted that in this case also, the irresistible amber of feminine attraction will prove its power, and draw this grass in the form of a Brahman any way it will, snapping like thread the resolution which would chain him to his muttering, as soon as it is seen.

And accordingly they drew up before them in a row the chorus of Indra's heavenly dancers. And they chose out of them all that Apsaras who seemed to them the least easily to be resisted, by

32

---

[1] *The wife of the sage Gautama, with whom Indra had an intrigue that covered him with shame, in more ways than one.*
[2] *'Chaturmukha.'*

reason of her rounded arms and dainty ankles, and sent her down to earth with suitable instructions, to seduce that Brahman from his muttering as quickly as she could. But she, to her amazement, found on her arrival, that, do what she might, she could not even so much as succeed in inducing him to look at her sideways even for a moment. So, after a while, she left him, and flew back to heaven in a pet. And they sent instead of her another, who presently returned, having found herself as ineffectual as the first. And they tried again, and sent, one after another, the whole of Indra's chorus, pelting as it were that stony-hearted old ascetic with a very shower of celestial flowers, and gaining the very opposite of the end at which they aimed. For inasmuch as he never ceased muttering even for a moment, all their efforts to corrupt him and reduce his stock of merit only added to its heap, making its mountainous proportions more formidable than before.

And finally Indra exclaimed in despair: We are conquered by this 'awatár' of obstinacy in the form of an ascetic, on whose rock the waves of this very sea of beauty beat in vain. And now there is no refuge for us but in the sole of the foot of the Burner[1] of the Bodiless God. For he alone is stronger than Love, whose power seems to fail us in this pinch, rendered nugatory by the intractable composition of this exasperating mutterer. And if even he can devise no remedy for this disease, it is incurable; and then will this incorruptible old devotee have us all at his mercy,[2] and bring heaven to its knees, and turn, if he pleases, the three worlds upside down.

[1] *i.e. Maheshwara himself, who burned Love with fire from his eye.*
[2] *Max Müller, to whom students of the Rig-Weda owe so much, was nevertheless essentially mistaken in saying that the word 'weda' means 'knowledge.' It does not mean knowledge, in our sense of the word, scientific, Baconian, Aristotelian; an idea quite alien to that of the old 'hotris.' By 'weda' they meant 'magical knowledge,' 'spells'; which being sung or muttered had power to compel the deities: thus the Brahman who possessed the 'knowledge' – in the phrase of the Brahmanas, 'yah ewam weda' – was the master of the world.*

And then, led by Indra, they came all together in a body to me; and placing the difficulty before me, they waited with anxiety to hear what I should say. And I looked there and then into the future, and saw in its dark mirror, like a picture, the ruin of that old ambitious Brahman, and the means by which it was destined to be accomplished. And after a while, I said slowly: All diseases are not able to be remedied by the same medicine, and notwithstanding the omnipotence of feminine attraction, this is a case wherein heavenly nymphs are impotent. and utterly without avail. For all these heavenly nymphs do nothing but dance and sing and attitudinise and ogle, imagining that as in the case of Menaká, Tilottamá, Rambhá, and the rest, they have only to show themselves to gain at once their end, trusting only to the body and its beauty, and very shallow coquetry and artifices to sharpen the edge of its effect, such as wind that stirs their clothing, or water that causes it to cling to the outline of their limbs and reveal, as if by accident, the thing that it pretends and is intended to conceal, and other such devices. But this Trishodadhi is a fish that, as I perceive, will not easily be caught by the bait of mere meretricious beauty, and in his case, the hook must be hidden in a lure of quite another kind. But there is a Daitya, named Aparapaksha,[1] living at the very bottom of the sea, who has a hundred daughters. And were beauty the necessary weapon in this instance, any one of them would serve the turn, since all of them have bodies formed as it were of ocean-foam, with lips of coral, and eyes like pools, and hair longer-than

[1] *i.e. the dark half of the lunar month.*

themselves, and voices like the echo of the waves; and only lately I heard them singing all together as I passed, on an island shore, and was myself all but bewitched, so that unawares I paused, hanging in the air to listen, waylaid as it were by the magic and the spell of that melancholy sound, forgetting my journey for the sake of their refrain. But now, since something more is necessary, you must abandon all the others, and betake you to the youngest of them all, who is rightly named Kalánidhi, though she is the ugliest and cleverest woman in the three worlds, for she is a very ocean of craft and trickery and guile,[2] and very knavish in disposition, as full of deception and caprice as the element in which she lives. And if you can get her to assist you, I do not doubt you will succeed. And perhaps, if you tell her that this is a matter in which all the heavenly nymphs have failed, she will help you out of spite; for she is very jealous of them all, and this is a glorious opportunity for her to show herself able to accomplish a thing which has baffled the ingenuity and beauty of everybody else. But certainly, if she either cannot or will not overcome this obstacle, I think that even the elephant-headed Lord of Obstacles himself would fail. For though beauty is a power stronger than any other, it may nevertheless sometimes be successfully resisted. But feminine ingenuity is a far more formidable antagonist, which no man has ever yet successfully encountered since the beginning of the world, since it is half protected by his own innumerable scruples in its favour, being utterly destitute of any sort of scruple of its own. And

[2]*There is a pun in her name, which as applied to the moon, means 'a store of digits,' but also signifies 'an ocean of wiles.'*

so, should Kalánidhi assist you, and fail after all, there is nothing to be done; and under the weight of this Brahman's mountain of accumulated merit, you must sink to the very bottom of the ocean of defeat, like an earth bereft of the tortoise to save it on its back.

CHAPTER IV

S O then, led by the lover of Ahalyá, the gods went off in a body to the bottom of the sea, to look for Kalánidhi, in such a hurry that they even forgot to worship me. And they found her father's residence, but not himself, for he happened to be away from home. And roaming here and there among his hundred daughters, all at once they came upon Kalánidhi, lying dreaming, curled in a bed formed by her own hair, in a giant oyster shell. And very suitable indeed seemed that shell to be her cradle, for her bosom resembled an enormous double pearl, not dead but living, keeping time slowly to the echo of the sea. And her body, that resembled a foaming wave, was hung all over with gems, picked up at random from the ocean floor, and her lips resembled sprigs that had fallen from the coral tree whose branches spread above her head in and out of the green water that moved her weedy tresses quietly to and fro. And as she opened her eyes and looked towards them, Indra said within himself: Maheshwara was right, and she is hideous, for all her beauty; for her eyes are like sea caves, out of which other eyes like those of an 'ajagara' seem to freeze you with their chill, and the smile on her thin lips resembles the sinister and silent laughter of a skull.

So as they came towards her, Kalánidhi gazed at them sleepily in wonder, and murmured softly to herself: What in the world can the gods want, so badly, as to bring them here, all together in a lump? For these must be the gods, since their eyelids do not wink. Something must surely have gone amiss in heaven, and beyond a doubt, sore indeed must be the need that drives them, for instead of sending Mátali, they have actually come themselves. And now it is very fortunate that my father is away. For he is far too simple[1] to drive a bargain with the gods, or anybody else, and would make no use of his opportunity.

And then she arose politely, and listened in silence, while Indra told her the whole story. And when he ended, she looked at him for a while ironically, and then she said: For centuries have we lived here, my father and my sisters and myself, and yet not even one of the gods ever visited us before. What honour, for a daughter of the Daityas! But what could be the services of such a thing as me, where even heavenly maidens fail? Moreover, I do not like cemeteries, seeing that every cemetery is the home of mouldering and evil-smelling bones and skulls, and flesh-eating Rákshasas and Wetálas and ghosts. But inasmuch as you have come here, not as friends or guests, but as merchants seeking to engage me in an enterprise for your own advantage, this is after all a matter on a mere commercial footing. And what then is to be the price of my assistance, and if I am successful, what is to be my appropriate reward?

Then said Maghawan:[1] I will give thee a crore of elephants, black as ink, with golden tusks; or if thou wilt, raiment woven out of the beams of the

[1] It is singular that Rákshasas in Hindoo story, like Ogres in the West, are always represented as simpletons and ninnies.

rising or the setting sun, or crystal vats of camphor strained from the midnight moon, or endless strings of jewels, or anything thou wilt. Then said Kalánidhi: What is the use of elephants, even black as ink with golden tusks, at the very bottom of the sea? And as for jewels, the sea floor is their very home, and I find them strewn at my very feet. And as for clothing, what do I want but my own hair? Then said Indra: Choose, then, for thyself, what I shall give thee. And Kalánidhi smiled. And she said: What if I were to require of thee a cushion, stuffed with the down that grows on the breast of Brahma's swan, or a fan, to cool me, made of the feathers of Saraswati's peacock's tail? And Indra said: Both shall be thine, and the bargain is complete. Then said Kalánidhi: Nay, there is no hurry. For what if I asked for a crore of crystal jars, filled to the very brim with 'amrita,' which, never having tasted, I am curious to taste? And Indra said: That also shall be thine, and so the bargain is complete. Then said Kalánidhi: Nay, for there might still be something lacking. What if I should say, that I long for a single blossom of Wishnu's 'párijáta' tree? For when I am in the cemetery, how should I endure to stay, even for a single moment, without its odour as an antidote to the reek of burning bodies and the stench of dying pyres? And Indra said: For that also I will answer, and now the bargain is complete. Then said Kalánidhi: Nay, be not hasty, in a matter of such importance. And now that I come to think of it, this Brahman must be very old and ugly. and exceedingly repulsive by reason of his long austerity. And what if I should ask thee for a lamp, that I might examine him from a distance, made of a single splinter chipped from Wishnu's 'kaustubha,' and filled not with oil, but the ooze of Shiwa's moon,

---

[1] *i.e. Indra.*

squeezed from the moonstones hanging on the trellises in Alaká, so that setting it in imitation of Maheshwara, like a diadem in my hair, I might be suitably equipped for reconnoitring your Brahman, in that gloomy home of ghosts? And Indra said: I will guarantee it thine, and the bargain is complete.

And then, Kalánidhi looked craftily at the eager god, out of the very corner of her eye. And all at once she began to laugh, and she exclaimed: Ha! lover of Ahalyá, thy need must surely be extreme, seeing that thou art as it seems ready to strip the very deities of their necessary attributes, to lure me to thy task. But now, learn that I did but play with thee and thy anxiety, to measure the degree of thy extremity; nor do I stand in need of any of those things that I have mentioned, nor of anything at all. For my assistance will be determined, not by bribes, but my own good pleasure and caprice. And it maybe I will go and try my skill against this old malignant mutterer, merely because I choose, and for no reward at all, and to show that I can be of use, when all the nymphs of heaven are more worthless than a straw. But in the meantime something more is necessary, without which I cannot even tell whether there is anything whatever to be done at all, even by myself. Tell me, then, the whole story of this Brahman, beginning from his very birth, omitting absolutely nothing; so that I may first of all discover, what is the strength or weakness of this enemy, whom thou wouldst have me engage and overthrow.

And Indra told her as she asked, beginning from the beginning, everything there was to know. And when he ended, Kalánidhi remained a while, buried in meditation. And suddenly she laughed, and said: O Maghawan, thy nymphs are surely very stupid, resembling beautiful bodies that are destitute of souls. Is it really possible that with such weapons in their hands, they could not so much as make the shadow of an impression on this Brahman? Come now, we will go together, for I shall need thee to assist me, and overthrow this mutterer, together with the mountain of his merit, by the favour of the Elephant-headed deity; for I think, that there will be very little difficulty in diverting his attention from his penance, after all: so little, that as I will show thee by experiment, it is not I that will upset him, but, aided by me, he will simply overturn himself. And when I have succeeded, I will ask thee for absolutely nothing in return; but thou shalt cause me to be worshipped by all the nymphs in heaven in a body, performing a 'pradakshina' around me in due form.

And Indra said within himself: Well said the Moony-crested, that jealousy alone would induce her to comply. And he exclaimed aloud, in an ecstasy of delight: O daughter of Aparapaksha, do but succeed in corrupting this ascetic, and I vow to thee, I will myself perform a 'pradakshina' about thee, at the head of all my nymphs!

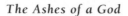

A FETTER OF THE SOUL

Up my longing eyes I tossed

Heaven to seek me in the skies:

Then I found them, and was lost

Gazing down, in other eyes.

But was it Heaven they found, or was it Hell?

Lord of the Moony Tire, I cannot tell.

Rudra

A FETTER OF THE SOUL

CHAPTER I

NOW in the meanwhile, Trishodadhi remained in that cemetery, in a posture of devotion. And as the interminable pattering of rain, drop after drop, fills up a lake, so did his everlasting muttering keep adding grain by grain to the mountain of his merit, till gazing at it, even Meru began to shudder for his own preeminence. And on he laboured diligently, pausing every now and then only when necessity compelled him to repair his rosary[1] of skulls, some of which from time to time wore out and fell to pieces, colliding with one another as he told them each in turn in the uninterrupted exercise of his devotions, till at length he sat surrounded by a very hill of bones, that resembled his own accumulated merit in another form. And sometimes, as he looked at them, he murmured to himself: Now, as it seems, the termination of my penance is approaching, and the beginning is drawing to an end, and very soon, I shall have amassed a suffient stock of merit to allow me to commence operations against the citadel of heaven, whose inhabitants are now at length beginning, not without a cause, to take fright at my proceedings, if I may form an opinion by their own. For not only did Indra come hither in person, and endeavour unsuccessfully to turn me from my purpose by offering me every

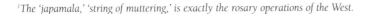
[1]*The 'japamala,' 'string of muttering,' is exactly the rosary operations of the West.*

kind of bribe, but latterly I have noticed heavenly maidens, coming, one by one, like a stream of stars falling from the sky, into this dismal earthly burning-ground, seeking to seduce me by their charms. But let them come, even all together; they shall find my resolution proof, and add against their will to the virtue they seek to undermine. Aye, my sublime determination is a rock, against which the sea of feminine cajolery shall hurl itself in vain.

So as he spoke, he struck violently one of his skulls against another, and it broke, and escaping from the string, rolled away out of his hand. And he raised his head, and cast a glance around him, with the object of discovering another to replace it. And as he did so, he started, and exclaimed within himself: Ha! just as I anticipated, there is as it seems yet another of these snares in the form of women, coming to entice me by the bait of her lascivious beauty, and hoping, more successful than her sisters, to roll my resolution, like a wheel, out of its deep and self-determined rut. But now, I will not even look at her at all. And very soon, growing like all her predecessors weary of the vain endeavour to attract my notice and distract my concentration, she will give it up of her own accord, and go back to her employers in disgust. And he stooped accordingly close over his beads, and muttered on, with his head bent towards the ground, and his eyes fixed on the broken skull within his hand, waiting to repair the injury till she should go away.

But in the meanwhile Kalánidhi, for she it was, having arrived at the cemetery, and exploring it, discovered Trishodadhi at his devotions, came, as he had perceived, close up to him, and standing just beside him, began to examine him attentively, like a general considering a fortress, in order to determine the proper method of attack. And after a while, she said softly to herself: Ha! very miserable indeed is this old skeleton of a Brahman, who, as he sits muttering, looks exactly like a number of the bones by which he is surrounded, that have somehow or other joined themselves together, and become tenanted by a passing disembodied soul. And little do I relish, as I look at him, the business I have in hand. But if I now abandon it, I shall become a laughing-stock, and they will think that I found myself unable to perform what I had promised, failing, like those miserable boobies, the heavenly nymphs, to keep my word. Moreover, the great in soul never dream of abandoning an enterprise, once they have begun it, till they have crowned it with success. And now, therefore, very soon it will be seen, which of us two, this loathsome old ascetic, or myself, will have to confess himself defeated, and give up his endeavour unachieved, like a bridge begun to span a great river that never reaches the farther shore. And she stopped to examine him, and said again: Doubtless, for all his busy muttering, he has long ago become aware of my presence, and as his attitude declares, is nerving himself for opposition and desperate resistance, expecting me to assault him point-blank, like all those very silly nymphs, by attitudinising, and giving him glimpses of my beauty, and practising other such tricks of coquetry before him. And beyond a doubt, he is flattering himself beforehand on his power of self-control, and already triumphing at the prospect of my ignominious defeat. But he will find himself very much mistaken, and unless I deceive myself, he will fall straight into the trap that I have set for him, never so much as suspecting it to be a trap at all, just because I shall set it where he is not looking for a snare. And to begin with, we shall see, whether even his curiosity will be proof. For I will take care to irritate and excite it, by doing all behind his back, so that he will not even be able to see anything at all, except by expressly turning round his head, which I imagine he will do, before very long. And he shall be attacked, not as he anticipates, but by that very avenue along which he least looks for danger, and one which, for all that, is the weakest and least guarded, and the best and the straightest way by which to reach and penetrate his soul – his ears. For sight can be assaulted only by what is present; but the ears are a passage by which I shall steal like a snake into the past, and pierce his very heart.

CHAPTER II

S O, then, as that suspicious yet unsuspicious old Brahman sat waiting, with his face turned towards the east, expecting every moment the assault of some temptation in the form of a sudden vision of intoxicating female beauty, time wore away, little by little, and hour succeeded hour, and he saw absolutely nothing. And the day slowly died, and the sun travelled onwards over his head, till his shadow crept silently from behind him and began to stretch out gradually longer and longer before his eyes. And as the sun set, the moon rose, and that cemetery became as it were a battleground in which the silver and the golden light engaged, and struggled silently for mastery; while night, their common enemy, took as it were advantage of their quarrel to bring up a host of shadows that threatened to destroy them both. And in the stillness of that epiphany of dusk, he listened, and heard absolutely nothing, but the beating of his own heart. And after a while, he said to himself: All is quiet in the forest: and now, as I thought, this last ineffectual temptress has taken herself off, having discovered the futility of her efforts to inveigle me, like all the rest before.

And at that very moment, he heard at a distance among the forest trees the noise of breaking branches, and the crashing of twigs and leaves. And he listened again, and said: Some large animal is forcing, as it seems, a way through the denseness of the wood, and coming gradually nearer. And he waited, and after a while, all at once there entered the cemetery from out of the wall of trees a tall royal elephant, with great yellow tusks that almost reached the ground. And he went slowly and wearily, for he seemed very old, and his skin hung in folds about him, and his body was all muddy, and crusted with the slime collected from the forest pools in which he wallowed, dried on him by the sun. And he came towards Trishodadhi, and passed him, paying absolutely no regard to him at all, and went wandering about here and there in the moonlight, as if he were looking in the cemetery for something that he could not find. And all at once, he stopped, close beside a pippala[1] tree, and spoke with a human voice, and said aloud in deep tones: O pippala, art thou at last the pippala I am looking for, or only a common tree?

And as Trishodadhi heard him, stupor came upon him, and he said to himself in amazement: Ha! what is this wonder, that an elephant should speak with an intelligible voice, and that I should understand him? And then, all at once, he exclaimed, in an ecstasy of delight: Ha! I understand. I can understand the language of the beasts. Now, beyond a doubt, this is a fruit of the tree of my asceticism, whose approaching term is the cause of my comprehension of his words. And his heart swelled with vanity and triumph, at the thought of his own forthcoming perfections. And as he listened eagerly for more, hardly crediting his own ears, which stood as it were on tiptoe with the intensity of their curiosity, all at once there came out of that pippala tree a voice. And it said, softly, like a sigh: O king of elephants, and art thou then the elephant at last, appointed me to meet?

And instantly, the elephant trumpeted with joy. And he exclaimed: O long-expected pippala, I could dance like a very peacock at the sight of thee! Can it be, and have I found thee?

---

[1] *The sacred fig, 'Ficus religiosa.' The word should be pronounced almost exactly like 'people' – dissyllabically.*

Then listen, without wasting any time, while I tell thee my story, and end it, and so at last free myself from the curse, and this hateful body of an elephant, in which I have been imprisoned for a 'yuga.'

Then said the pippala: O elephant, thy voice is very loud. Dost thou not see that old ascetic, sitting plunged in meditation, surrounded by a heap of bones, whose soul is doubtless absent far away, on some celestial errand? Know, that I love him, for year by year I have watched him sitting by me as I grew, almost as motionless as I myself: and I will not have his soul disturbed. Moreover, if thy tones disturb him, he will probably awake in wrath, and lay on thee another curse. Come round me, therefore, to my other side, and let my trunk conceal thee, and screen thy harsh voice; and do thou speak very low. And the elephant obeyed, doing as the pippala said. But Trishodadhi, when he heard it, almost abandoned the body in vexation. And he said within himself: Out upon this pippala, and her affection for myself! Now, very probably, I shall not hear. And he strained his ears to catch, if possible, the matter of their conversation, utterly forgetting to mutter, for the time.

Then said the elephant: O holy tree, the sight of thee is like water to one dying in the sand. For long ago, when I fell into this form, by reason of a curse, pronounced upon me for a sin, this meeting with thyself was fixed as the termination of the curse. And I have wandered up and down, as I think for a very 'kalpa,' asking

every pippala that I saw the very question that never received an answer till this moment; so that, hearing it, I almost leaped out of the body in my joy. Now listen, and so at last, emerging from this dungeon of an elephant, I shall again become a man, as soon as I have told thee of my crime; since this is the condition of the fulfilment and abolition of the curse.[1] Then the pippala sighed again: Dear elephant, speak lower, lest the end of one curse be only the beginning of another, in perhaps a lower form than thine. And Trishodadhi, as he listened, shook with anger and irritation. And the elephant said: O pippala, I will do my best. But this voice of mine is my natural tone, appointed for my species. And after all, I do not think it will disturb the sage. For though his body is so near us, it never moves, and beyond a doubt his soul is far away, attending to its own affairs. And how, then, should the empty body overhear us, in the absence of its soul?

CHAPTER III

ND the pippala said: Speak on. Then said the elephant: O pippala, know, that long ago, in my former birth, I was a king, named Ruru. And I had for my minister, a Brahman, named Trishodadhi. And he had an incomparable wife, by name Watsatarí, a very paragon of beauty and devotion to her husband.[2] And she it was, whose virtue was the cause of my falling into this body of an elephant, by reason of a curse.

 50

[1] *This, though strange to Western modern ears, would be quite familiar to an old Hindoo. All these 'curses' had their 'termination' definitely assigned to them – ' áwadhi' – exactly as in the text, deliverance being made conditional on the telling of the tale.*

[2] *The name, par excellence. of a model Hindoo wife is 'patidewatá,' 'patiwratá': i.e. 'she to whom her husband is a god.' This epithet is the Victoria Cross, the blue ribbon of the Indian matron.*

So as he spoke, the heart of Trishodadhi, as he listened, almost jumped from his body with amazement. And he said to himself: Ha! what! Am I dreaming, or can it actually be, that this is my old master, King Ruru, in the semblance of an elephant? And suddenly, that old life which he had so long forgotten and abandoned, rose up and stood before him, like a picture in a dream. And like a flash of lightning, he flew back into the past. And all at once, a pang shot into his heart, keen as long ago, at that moment of intolerable agony, when he looked and saw his wife, for the very last time, in the arms of the King. And suddenly, a thirst like fire rose up out of his soul, and took him by the throat. And he gasped, not knowing what he did, and at that moment, wonder changed into a very fever of fierce curiosity, and he murmured to himself: Ha! what! Was she then, after all, not guilty, but as he says virtuous? Ha! then, now I shall discover the whole truth, and learn, what I never knew, the story of her fall, if indeed she fell, and what occurred after I went away, never so much as bidding her farewell.

And lo! strange! as he thought of her again, there ran as it were a sword into his soul. And like flame, that suddenly bursts out anew in the ashes of a fire extinct, so all at once grief, and fierce regret, and a passionate yearning for the wife that played him false, surged and struggled in the dark oblivion of his ocean of recollection, so that he swayed and tottered as he sat. And utterly forgetting all, he let his rosary suddenly drop out of his hand, and turned abruptly round, to see as well as hear. And when he looked, he saw the elephant, standing still with drooping ears, leaning against the pippala's trunk. And then again, no sooner had he turned, than he exclaimed within himself: Ha! now again, I have come within a little of spoiling all, by betraying to them that I am a party to their interview, and moreover, not a bystander indifferent, but one very much concerned indeed. And instantly he turned back, resuming his old attitude, and remained, still as a tree, almost dying with apprehension, lest he should lose even a single word of their discourse.

So as he sat listening, all at once the pippala said: O king of elephants, why, after commencing thy narration, hast thou suddenly broken off, no sooner than begun? Then the elephant sighed deeply. And he said: Holy tree, I stopped, as it were against my will, at the thought of her innocence, and my own evil conduct, and the terrible retribution, that overtook me in the shape of this elephant's skin, which is as it were nothing but the consequence of my own works in a brutal form. Truly have the sages said: What is the cause of the misery of soul, if not the envelope of body? And whence arises the envelope of body, but from works? And from what do works originate, if not from passion, and this again, from pride, itself the fruit of the tree of a want of discrimination, and the black night of ignorance? Alas! while I thought myself a king, what was I but a chip, tossed upon the waves of time; a very bubble, rolling from side to side, like the drop of rain water on the leaf of a blue lotus; more momentary

52

than the lightning playing on the clouds; unsubstantial, fleeting, and unsteady as the shadow of a foolish moth, fluttering about the flame of a flickering torch agitated by sighing gusts of wind?

Then said the pippala: O elephant, thou speakest the very truth; nevertheless, thy reflections only delay the progress of the tale, and thy own release from the very thing that thou deplorest; and at this rate, the sun will return to us long before thy story is half told. And the elephant said: Pippala, I have done. Listen, then, to the story of my crime, and may its memory desert me, together with this skin of a forest elephant, as soon as it is told. For even the body of a brute is not so great a punishment to the evil-doer, as the remorse which never leaves him, in the form of the recollection of his crime.

CHAPTER IV

OR long ago, being, as I told thee, a king, named Ruru, I was married in my youth to a queen. And she was beautiful, with a beauty that resembled the beauty of a panther, for it was fierce and spotted and treacherous and crafty, and I was a prey to it, for I was very young, and I knew not anything of woman but her shell. And I was devoted to my wife, and trusted her implicitly, and had never suspected her fidelity even in a dream. And I returned suddenly one evening at nightfall into my palace, and looked, and lo! she was fondling another man, a Rajpoot, whom she had brought into the palace through a window by a ladder, having fallen in love with him as she saw him in the street.

So when I saw her, I uttered a cry, and stood. But they, seeing me, separated like a flash of lightning, and fled, he back into the street, and she to her own apartments. And where he went, or what she did, I know not. But when the dawn was breaking, I looked, and again I saw her coming back with stealthy step. And all at once, as she came, she looked, and saw me standing, exactly where I stood before, never having moved, all night long. And instantly, she stopped short, and gazed at me with eyes that were filled with amazement, which changed, as I watched her, into the extremity of fear. And all at once, I uttered a terrible cry. And instantly she sank to the ground, bereft of reason. But I turned, and ran away, and went out into the street.

And I wandered up and down in the darkness that was just becoming daylight, with a soul on fire, not knowing where I went or what I did; and I came suddenly upon a miserable wretch in ragged garments, and I said to him: Change now very quickly thy garments for my own. And he, looking at me, very rapidly agreed, and we changed, and I gave him all my jewels, and put on his very loathsome rags; and so he went away. And I said to myself: Now will I leave my palace and my kingdom, and become a 'sannyási,' turning my back upon the world. And lo! almost as I spoke, another man suddenly came upon me, a little old man with grey

hair that escaped from his handkerchief,[1] and keen eyes like those of a weasel. And he said to me: Ha! night-walker, who art thou? And I laughed, guessing him to be a thief; and I said: Maharáj,[2] I am a robber, like thyself. Then said that old man: I am the chief of all the robbers in this city, and I know thee not. And I said: How shouldst know me, who am but just arrived in the city, having fled here by reason of trouble in my own? And he said: Wilt thou come and be of mine? And I said: Aye! with thee or any other rascal. What does it matter? And I laughed in bitterness, not caring if I died. Then that little old man came up close, and looked at me narrowly for a while; and he said: Thou art very young and handsome, and as I think, no thief at all. And whence comes the trouble of the young but from women? And I said: O king of robbers, thou art subtle; for I am indeed the victim of a woman, and my life is at an end.

And then suddenly, that strange old man struck me a blow with his open hand upon my shoulder, so hard, that it hurt. And he exclaimed: Fool! art thou actually grieving for the loss of a woman? What! dost thou not know, that he who loses one, can find without any difficulty a hundred other women, just as good or better than herself? And as he spoke, all at once I began to laugh, and as I laughed, I cried. And I exclaimed: Ha! old thief, I am obliged to thee; and like a good physician, thou hast cured my malady, with words that are sharper than a knife. But beware! for if I ever meet thee again, I will have thee thrown to be trampled by an elephant.

[1] *i.e. the 'roomal' or 'paggri,' on the head: one of the two essential garments of the Hindoo; used by the Thags as a strangling noose.*
[2] *This term, properly applied to a king, is by politeness or irony also used much as we use 'Sir.'*

And then I turned my back upon him, and went away, and left him standing, saying to myself as I went: He is right. And now, then, I will go back into my palace, and make all the other women in the three worlds pay for the conduct of my wife. Ha! I should indeed have been a fool, to become a 'sannyási,' for such a thing as her; and this old rascal has raised me as it were from the dead, and replaced the 'danda'[1] in my hand.

And then, O pippala, as I said, so I did. And laying the burden of the state upon the shoulders of my minister, Trishodadhi, I ran wild among the women of my kingdom, and I became an object of dread to every one of my subjects that had either a daughter or a sister or a wife.

And as he listened, Trishodadhi said within himself: Aye! robber of a king, so it was; and little dost thou dream how close to thee is a living witness to the truth of thy words. And all forgetful of his muttering, he listened eagerly for the remainder of the tale.

CHAPTER V

 ND the elephant said: Pippala, as it happened, I had for my 'wita'[1] a very incarnation of malignity and craft, on whom I laid the duty of discovering every woman in my kingdom or elsewhere, whose beauty might make her worthy of my regard. And this wita, while bringing to my notice every day the treasures of others, never told me of his

[1] *i.e. the rod of punishment, one of the essential attributes of a king.*
[1] *The function of the wita in old Hindoo courts was analogous to that of Chiffinch in 'Peveril of the Peak.'*

own, but kept me scrupulously ignorant. But one day there came to me one of his agents, to whom he had done some injury or other, and he said: O Maharáj, thy wita is offering thee husks, and keeping back the kernel; possessing as he does a daughter more beautiful than the moon. And hearing this, I flew into a rage. And I sent for the wita, and compelled him, under penalty of death, to produce his daughter; and I took her away from him, disregarding all his prayers. So at last, finding all his supplications useless, all at once that wita yielded, and acquiesced in his dishonour, like an elephant tamed. Ha! had I only known him, I should have put him instantly to death; for he was but waiting till he saw his opportunity. And the consequence of my action in this matter of the wita and his daughter lay waiting: till the time came, when it rose up suddenly like a cobra, and bit me in the heel.

But in the meantime, careless of the wita and his vengeance, I lived like a mad bee, intent upon nothing but ruining the lotuses that I rifled of their honey, remaining beside each, only so long as was necessary to destroy it, after sipping its sweet. And gradually my kingdom began to assume the semblance of a garden, in which every tree was mourning, bewailing the fate of its loveliest blossoms, which lay on the ground, trampled as it were into the mud. Enough! for why should I detain thee, and delay my own emancipation from this carcase of an elephant by enumerating details that are not to the point. Know, that there came a day, when having left as usual the burden of the kingdom on the shoulders of my minister, I went out into the forest to hunt. And after a while, growing weary of the chase, I dismissed my attendants, and came slowly home alone, wandering after them on foot. And I lingered as I went, listening to the noise of the canes, singing in the breeze; aye! well do I remember the music that they made, as if prognosticating by their exquisite melody the sweetness of the meeting that was just on the very point of crossing my steps, to plunge my soul, in the twinkling of an eye, as it were into a vat, and change its dye, turning it first into red, and finally into deep and inalterable blue.[1]

For as I rambled slowly on, it happened, by destiny's decree, that a necklace of great pearls, that I always wore around my neck, its clasp coming open, slipped off, and fell upon the ground. And at that very moment, a bird of the race of hawks pounced suddenly upon it, and carried it away, attracted by its glitter, or who knows? For I think that the very god of Love took, it may be, that form of a bird, to bring about his end. And I ran after it, as it were awaking from my musing, with a shout, and the bird, after flying a little way, becoming frightened, or it may be, by express design, let fall the necklace from his claws, and flew away. And seeing it fall, I ran towards it, and all at once, I found my way blocked by a very high wall, on the farther side of which the necklace fell. And I went up to that wall, and as I did so, I listened, and heard the noise of steps beyond the wall. And instantly I called aloud: O thou, whoever thou art, beyond the wall, know, that the necklace is mine. And hearing no answer, I looked about, and seeing a tree standing near,

[1] *Red is the colour of affection, and blue that of its highest power, devotion that is immortal and indelible.*

I swung myself up, by means of its branches, upon the wall, and looked over. And when I did so, lo! there below me in the garden stood a young woman, looking up towards me; and on the ground was the necklace, lying at her very feet.

And as I looked down at her, O pippala, all at once the necklace, the very object of my coming, vanished clean out of my mind, obliterated in an instant, and swept into oblivion by the wonder of her eyes. And yet it was not merely their beauty that amazed me, pools of lapis lazuli though they were, to whose brink that bird had brought me, as if to drown me, dizzy at their very depth. But strange! fixed as they were, upturned towards me, bent and as it were pointed full upon my own, they never wavered, and I was puzzled by their gaze. For there was no curiosity at all in them, nor any trace of timidity or fear, far less of challenge, or anger, or agitation, or any tumult of emotion, but rather an ocean, and as it were an atmosphere of silence, and shadowy peace, and a spirit of unutterable quiet and repose, like that of some unviolated water, bound by a spell of secrecy and lying hidden in the middle of a forest, on whose dark film the dead leaves lie, unmoved by animals that drink, or winds that blow. And so little did I seem to be the target of those motionless unfathomable eyes, that I would have turned my head, to discover what thing other than myself it was that she regarded, but that I could not look away from them at all. And she stood with her head, a little bent, like one that listens rather than that looks, and thrown just a very little back upon her

shoulders, so that all unknown to her the round bosses of her wide and glorious bosom stretched out and up towards me, as if dying to express that curiosity and agitation which was wanting in her eyes, while her slender figure, like a stalk, stood still and seemed to sway, as if with anxiety, lest the weight that it supported should snap it in the middle. And as I sat gazing, lost in a sea of perplexity and admiration, all at once she spoke, and said in a low voice that resembled a caress rendered audible to the ear: Who art thou, if, as I guess, thou hast climbed upon the wall, and what is thy intention?

And I said, with confusion and surprise: I came upon the wall, O lady of the lovely eyes, to recover yonder necklace which is lying at thy feet. Then she said: Dost thou see it lying? And I said: Surely I see it very plainly, as thou dost also. Then she said: Come down, then, and take it, and begone. For I cannot do it for thee, seeing that I am blind.

And Trishodadhi, as he listened, groaned within himself. And he murmured: Aye! indeed! alas! so she was; and these were her very eyes: and now well I know that the story of this elephant is true. And all oblivious of his muttering, he listened to the tale.

CHAPTER VI

AND the elephant said: Pippala, when I heard her, I came within a little of falling from the wall, struck by the shock of pity and amazement at her words. And I exclaimed: Blind, O thou beautiful and unfortunate! But thou art surely jesting. What! can such eyes as thine, more lovely than the pool in which the lotuses delight, O, which put to shame the very heaven at midnight with its stars, be really blind? And she said, quietly: Yet is it as I say. And I struck my hands together, and groaned aloud, almost weeping, for remorse and despair. And I exclaimed: Out, out on the Creator, who could be guilty of so criminal a blunder as to make such eyes as thine, and yet forget to give them sight, which he has been so careful to remember in the case of every common eye! Then she said gently: Nay, utter no blame of the Creator. Blame rather me myself, since doubtless this my blindness is a punishment deserved, for sins committed by myself, in some forgotten former birth, and the fruit of a tree I and no other planted. Or rather, blame not anything at all, since thy business is neither with my eyes, nor me, at all, but rather with thy necklace. Come, as I said, and take it quickly, and begone.

And I looked at her for a moment in agitation, and I said, with emphasis: Take thou the necklace; it is no longer mine, having fallen at the feet of its proper owner: and wise was the bird that

stole it from me, to lay it where it is. This only I regret that alas! thou canst not see it, for it is worthy of beauty such as thine. And she smiled, looking at me, as it were, with those eyes that did not falter, and she said: Stranger, what have I to do with thee or with thy necklace? Come, now, cease talking nonsense on the wall, to one that must not listen; but take thy necklace and begone.

O pippala, I know not if I tell thee what befel, so as to make thee comprehend. But know, that in that moment since I came upon the wall, I was changed. For her voice completed what her eyes began, and her smile took my heart and set it shaking like a leaf with an ecstasy of rapture and anxiety, causing me to tremble with so violent an agitation that I could hardly keep my place upon the wall. And I knew that I was looking at a woman of a kind that I had never seen before, and I tossed away my past in the twinkling of an eye. And I said to myself, quivering with the extremity of delight and the fever of determination: Ha! then as it seems, destiny waited till this moment, to show me perfection in the form of the woman of my dreams. And what! O thou matchless, intoxicating beauty, now that I have found thee, dost thou bid me go away, and leave thee as soon as found? Nay, nay; not for the three great worlds with all that they contain, will I consent ever to part from thee again. And now, thou shalt be my wife and queen, whether thou wilt or no.

And at that moment, I think that the very god of Love himself put a thought into my heart. And I looked at her with fierce affection,

as she stood waiting quietly below, and said softly to myself: I will stay, O peremptory beauty, in despite of thee, and all the powers of earth and heaven combined. And I said to her aloud: Since then I must, and thou permittest, I will descend, and take it, and begone. And I leaped from the wall towards her, awkward by express design, intending to feign injury to myself, and with so good a will, that as it happened, I actually did the very thing I meant to feign. And fell heavily, bruising my foot upon the ground beside her, so that she drew back in alarm. And I uttered a moan that was anything but feigned. And immediately she said, with commiseration in her voice: Alas! now I fear my impotence has been a cause of injury to thyself. Art thou hurt? And I said: Nay, it is nothing. Let me rest for but a moment, and so I will depart. And she hesitated, and said with indecision: This is a misfortune and a difficulty. For I know thee not, being utterly in the dark about thee; and I dare not stay beside thee, not knowing who thou art. And yet, if thy voice is any indication of thy quality, I think I need not fear thee. And I said hastily: Fear absolutely nothing; and I will tell thee my family and name, in exchange for thy own. And easy is it to perceive that thou art no common person's wife. Then she said: I am called Watsatarí, and my husband is the minister of the king, of whom doubtless thou hast heard,[1] since everybody knows him, not only in this city, but elsewhere.

And once again I started and exclaimed: What! the wife of Trishodadhi? Then she said: I see, thou knowest. And I said again: What! can it be?

[1] *A Hindoo woman will never mention her husband's name. They allude to him in terms that correspond to the Latin 'iste,' 'ille.'*

And once again I started and exclaimed: What! the wife of Trishodadhi? Then she said: I see, thou knowest. And I said again: What! can it be! Trishodadhi? And as I spoke, I looked at her in absolute dismay. And I murmured to myself: Alas! alas! Had she only been the wife of any other husband in the three wide worlds, only not of him.

And Trishodadhi, as he listened, exclaimed within himself: Ah! yes, indeed; thou art right. Had it only been any other husband than myself, indeed it had been well. And oblivious of his muttering, he listened in agitation to the tale.

CHAPTER VII

ND the elephant said: Pippala, as I gazed at her, struck by the thunderbolt of astonishment and dismay, my heart smote me: for all unintentionally, I found myself playing the traitor to my minister, and becoming, as indeed I was already, the worshipper of his wife. And well I knew, that love would prove stronger than gratitude, and more powerful than friendship, and that he was already doomed. And I said to myself: Ha! now destiny and the deity of Love have combined, to throw me, as it were against my will, into the company of one whom I had determined to avoid, and are driving me to injure, one, whom I would rather wish to honour and regard. But now it is too late, and well I see, that will happen which must happen, and she and I and her husband are but puppets, dancing to the bidding of powers that are greater than our own. And once again I murmured: Watsatarí; Trishodadhi; it cannot be. Then she said: Who art thou, to be so well acquainted, as it seems thou art, both with my husband and myself, and what is there in the circumstances that arouses in thee such surprise?

And as I looked at her, I trembled, saying to myself: Now perhaps it is as well, she cannot see. And now I dare not tell her who I am, for that would be utter ruin, since doubtless rumour has told her all about me. And I thought for a moment, and then all at once I laughed aloud. And I exclaimed: O wife of Trishodadhi, if one should have commissioned thee, saying, Go at dead of night to the very middle of the sea, and there catch in its immensity a single little mina[1] that has swallowed such-and-such a ring; and thou going accordingly and grasping blindly in its water shouldst find that very fish enclosed in thy hand, say, would it not surprise thee also, to find chance putting into thy clutch a thing no ingenuity could ever have discovered? And she said with a smile: Who then is the fish; is it I, or is it he? And I said: It is thy own pretty neck which is the fish; for yonder necklace was commissioned to encircle it. And now let me tell thee, since I see thou art suspicious of myself, fearing no doubt the anger of thy husband, should he discover thee in my society, that he would hardly have excused thee for sending me away, as presently he himself will tell thee, as soon as he returns. For know that I am a Rajpoot, and the confidential

[1] *A kind of fish.*

agent of a neighbouring king, to whom thy husband lately rendered by his policy an inestimable service. And since he absolutely refused reward, the king my master said to me: Gratitude, like a river, dammed in one direction, will find an outlet in another; and since I may do nothing for Trishodadhi, I will at least do something for his wife. For I have heard, that she is of incomparable beauty. Take, then, this necklace, and answer for its safety with thy head. And ride night and day, going towards the capital of Ruru, and seek out his minister, and ask for Watsatarí his wife. And when she is actually before thee, put with thy own hands the necklace on her neck, and say: King Chandradatta bids thee know, by this emblem, that the chain of obligation to thee and to thy husband is on his neck, and when there is a difficulty, send him this; and he will overcome it. And now, right glad I am to find thee; for I have not slept since I started, for fear of losing the necklace, and forfeiting my head. And surely the bird which filched it from me to carry it to thee was some deity in disguise; for how could a mere bird know, for whom it was designed? So take thou the necklace, and when thy husband sees it, summon me: and I will tell him also, and depart.

And she listened attentively, looking as it were straight at me as I lied, till I trembled, rejoicing, and yet hardly crediting, that she could not see me; and when I ended, she stood meditating, while I watched her, in ecstasy at having hit upon a clever lie, by means of which I hoped to prolong our conversation, and look at her with

impunity, careless of what might come of it at last. And presently she said: Where then is the necklace? And I placed it in the lotus of the hand she held toward me, stealing guilty undetected glances at her creeper of an arm; and she took it, and felt it all over, telling every pearl, exactly as yonder old ascetic told his beads as I passed him; while I stood gazing at her, hardly able to draw breath, And after a while she said: Surely these pearls are very large? And I said: There are no others equal to them, even in the sea. And she sighed a very little, and she said with regret: Their beauty is for other eyes than mine. And I watched her eagerly, saying to myself: Ha! can it be that this delicious beauty resembles all her far inferior sisters, and is tempted by the pearls she cannot see? O pippala, I tell thee, that though it made for my advantage, it was a grief to me to find her, as I thought, like other women. Ha! but I did her wrong, and did not know her, for she had something in her soul that I did not understand.

And all at once, half, as I conjectured, in derision, and half, it may be, tempted by the shadow of a wish to try them on her neck, she took the necklace by both ends in her hands, and hung it up around her throat, letting those lucky pearls rest for a single instant on the margin of her swelling breast. And utterly bewildered, instantly I forgot my self-control. And I stepped forward, saying hastily: Nay, thou dost not know the secret of its clasp. And before she could prevent me, for blind as she was, she knew not what I meditated, I put my two arms, that trembled with

intoxication and timidity, and wonder at their own audacity, suddenly around her neck, and took the two ends of the necklace in my hands, and placing them together, was just about to clasp them. And at that very moment, I looked, and lo! there, at a distance in the garden, stood Trishodadhi her husband, looking at me with eyes that resembled caverns, filled with black and shining water in the form of unutterable despair.

And Trishodadhi, as he listened, groaned within himself, writhing as he sat at the reminiscence of that moment, which shot into his heart like a flame. And utterly oblivious of his muttering, he listened eagerly for the remainder of the tale.

CHAPTER VIII

ND the elephant said: Pippala, when my eyes met his, I stood absolutely still, like a bird fascinated by the glare of a snake, altogether forgetting what it was that I was doing, and what it was that I was holding in my arms. And all at once he turned and went away, without ever looking round. And at that very instant Watsatari, all ignorant of his presence and the cause of my behaviour, pushed me suddenly away, with such force as all but to overthrow me. And as I gazed at her like one dreaming, intent on nothing but her husband's interruption, I saw an angry flush rise like dawn upon her face, and standing like a queen, she knitted her bow-like brows in wrath, and exclaimed, in a voice that shook with indignation: Dastard, dost thou dare to take such cowardly advantage of my incapacity? Get thee gone, and approach me, if at all, at the bidding of my husband. And she took the necklace, and tearing it from her neck, still unfastened as it was, she threw it violently away, not caring where it fell. And I in my agitation, cowed by her vehemence and the apparition of her husband, instantly obeyed her. And I exclaimed: O wife of Trishodadhi, thou art mistaken and unjust, but I obey thee. And I climbed the wall, not so much as even remembering the necklace, and hastened home, saying to myself: Now, very likely, he will kill her. And if so, I myself shall miserably perish, unable to endure my life without her; and what is to be done? And I sent hastily, as soon as I arrived, for Trishodadhi, not knowing what to say to him when he should arrive. But very soon my messengers returned, saying: Maharáj, Trishodadhi is nowhere to be found. And I sent them back, with orders to bring him as soon as he could come. And all that night I waited in anxiety, sleepless, haunted by the picture of Watsatarí, and fearing for her life. Then in the morning, those messengers returned again, saying: Maharáj, Trishodadhi has disappeared; and no one can tell us anything about him, or whither he has gone.

So when I heard it, I said within myself: Now, beyond a doubt, he has hidden himself somewhere, fearing for his life. And I sent everywhere to search for him; and in the meanwhile, I went back secretly once more to that garden, and climbed upon the wall, only

to find it empty, for Watsatarí was gone. And after a while I came away, sick with disappointment, only to discover that still Trishodadhi was nowhere to be found. And so for many days it continued; and every day I went in vain to look for Watsatarí in the garden, and it seemed as though Trishodadhi and she had plotted to disappear together, without leaving any trace. But after a while, finding by inquiry that the wife of Trishodadhi was looking for him, exactly like myself, I sent her a message from the King, saying: Thy husband has vanished, and much I fear, that some enemy has made away with him, leaving the affairs of my kingdom in confusion, for want of his sagacity. But know, that I am moving heaven and earth to find him, and do not be alarmed. For it may be that he is absent in pursuit of some object of his policy, of his own accord.

And then at last, parched with intolerable thirst, and unable any longer to endure separation from its cause, I went one day as usual to the garden, and mounted on the wall, and looked. And lo! there she was again, looking up towards me on the wall, and listening, exactly as she did before. And at the sight of her, my heart almost leaped out of my body with delight. And instantly, without waiting for permission, I sprang from the wall, and went towards her; and as I did so, something moved under my foot. And I looked, and it was the necklace, that had lain there where she threw it, ever since. And I left it lying, and exclaimed: O wife of Trishodadhi, as it appears, I have discovered thee at last. Listen now, without losing any time; and even as it is, I fear, lest we should be overheard by spies. And she said quietly: What is the matter? Then I said: Thou knowest that thy husband has been missing, ever since I saw thee first. And she said: I know. Then I said: Dost thou know where he is gone? And she said: No. And I said: I am here to tell thee. For no sooner had I left thee than I went to him; and I found him on the very point of setting out upon a journey. And I told him of our meeting in the garden; and he listened, and when I ended, he said quickly: This is no time for necklaces of pearls. For know, that I have just discovered, by certain information, that King Ruru, having somehow or other cast eyes upon my wife, has fallen so violently in love with her, that he cannot even sleep. And well I know what he will do, since only too often has he exhibited specimens of his behaviour, in the case of other wives than mine. And therefore, while yet time suffers, I am escaping, since if he catches me, well he knows, and I know, that he will catch Watsatarí as well. For where I am, she will be also, seeing that a good wife such as she is cannot desert her husband, even in a dream. But if, as I am now about to do, I can only place myself beyond his reach, she also will be safe. For he will not dare openly to carry her away, at least for a little while, and in the interval, I will remove her secretly myself. And now the deity has sent thee to me, in the very nick of time; and I place her in thy hands, more valuable than any necklace. Go to her quickly, for no one will suspect thee, and bring her, telling absolutely no one, for I cannot trust any of my household, who fear the king, and are, it may be, in his pay. But thou shalt help me to cheat him of his prey. And then he told me of his hiding-place, and went away; and ever since, I have sought thee in this garden, day by day, striving to discover thee, without letting any even of his household know. And now at last I find thee, and nothing more remains, but to make arrangements, how and when I shall come to thee, to carry thee away. And now, delay not, for the king's eye is on thee; and every future hour may be too late. And the very necklace may be to thee a pledge of my fidelity. For yonder it lies, exactly where it fell from thy hand, though I had only to lift it, to carry it away and make it mine.

And Trishodadhi, as he listened, ground his teeth together, and exclaimed within himself: Ah! perjured king and royal liar, well didst thou deserve to fall, not only into that body of an elephant, but something lower still.

CHAPTER IX

AND the elephant said: Pippala, when I ended, all at once that lady of the steady eyes laughed as it were in my very face. And while I stood confounded and astounded by her laughter, which poured from her like a stream, she broke off abruptly, and she said: O King Ruru, I congratulate thee from my heart on thy extraordinary talent for deceit. And I waited, just to hear what further artifice thou hadst

concocted, in order to beguile me. And I admire thy roguery, and as I think, King Bhartrihari[1] was but a novice in comparison with thee, such a master art thou of thy trade, and all the arts of cozening my sex. But now, cease wallowing like a hog in the mire of lying and deceit, and tell me truly, what thou hast done with my husband. For know, that thou wouldst never have found me here to-day to meet thee, but for my determination to ask of thee this very question. Hast thou murdered him, or stolen him away, or what?

And as she spoke, I staggered, like one that has received a blow. And I ejaculated: O lady, art thou dreaming, or what is this delusion? And then, angrily she stamped her little foot upon the ground. And she said sternly, yet with derision: O King, has not thy own experience yet taught thee, that kings are harder to conceal than the very sun at noon? And has thy dealing with such multitudes of women not yet shown thee, that even a king, versed in trickery and every diplomatic art, might take lessons in intrigue from any woman, aye, even from so incomplete a specimen of womankind as me? Hast thou allowed thyself to be outwitted even by the blind? And she laughed, while I gazed at her, astounded by her exaltation, arising like a storm in such gentleness as hers, and helpless in my anger, which was impotent, being swallowed by admiration for her beauty and her craft. And presently she said: What! art thou dumb at last, and has thy voluble eloquence deserted thee, when truth was wanted rather than a lie? Know, that I suspected thee, from the very first, for thy voice betrayed thee,

[1]*The aphorisms of this king. who according to tradition combined the usually incompatible professions of king, poet, grammarian, gay Lothario, and sage, are household words in India.*

carrying in it as it were an echo of command. And for this very reason was it that I fingered thy necklace, by express design, to ascertain whether thou wert speaking truth about its value. And I said privately to myself, as I handled it: This is surely the ornament of no other than a king. And as to thy story of the bird that brought it hither, well I understand that it was a fable, like thy fish; and thy necklace was nothing but a snare, by means of which thou didst hope to bribe me, cunning in thy knowledge of my sex. And thereafter, all unknown to thee, I caused myself to be carried in a palanquin, a day or two ago, where I could listen to the voice of the king, and lo! it was thy own. So drop thy mask, for it is only too transparent, since even the blind can easily see through it. And tell me, what hast thou done with my husband? Hast thou murdered the husband, as a stepping-stone to the embraces of the wife?

And I said hastily: O admirable lady, I swear to thee, that I am as innocent of thy husband's disappearance as thyself. Nay, I have striven to discover him, without avail, and his going is a mystery I cannot fathom. Then she said: Thou art prevaricating, and if thou art ignorant of the reason of his absence, I am not. For certain I am, that it is somehow or other connected with thy design upon myself, with which it coincides in the time of its occurrence, though I cannot understand it.

Pippala, as she spoke, I wondered at her sagacity, for blind as she was, not having seen him as I did in the garden, she came within but a little of the truth. And I said: Watsatarí, I swear to thee, that thy husband has made himself invisible absolutely of his own accord, and I am absolutely guiltless of any practices against him, as indeed my kingdom suffers by his absence. Then she said: Partly I believe thee, though not relying on thy own asseveration. For thou hast forfeited all claim to be believed, in anything whatever. But even if thou hast not actually removed him, thy action it is, which has driven him away. For beyond a doubt, he must somehow or other have penetrated thy design, and gone away accordingly, and O that this may be all. For bitterly do I reproach myself, for having, in a moment of curiosity, lent a colour to his suspicion; and even though he was not there, yet as thou didst place thy arms about my neck, on pretext of fastening the necklace, taking a cowardly advantage of my impotence of sight, I felt myself a criminal. And when he comes again, I will confess it, and take his forgiveness for my fault, into which I fell by my own blindness, and thy abominable treachery.

And Trishodadhi, as he listened, exclaimed within himself: Ha! very wonderful is the intuition of women pure in soul; for she hit upon the very truth. Ah! that I should have doubted her, even in a dream! And oblivious of his muttering, he listened to the tale.

CHAPTER X

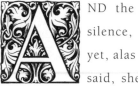ND the elephant said: Pippala, I gazed at her in silence, utterly unable to find anything to say. And yet, alas for her! convicted as I was, by everything she said, she did but add to the volume of my passion, like one that pours oil upon a flame. For her anger and her grief and her repentance, and her extraordinary subtlety, only made her more beautiful than ever, and my own evil conduct resembled the radiance of a lamp, that was thrown back from the opal of her purity in showers of incomparable colour on myself. And all at once she seated herself upon the ground. And she said: Stand thou there before me, and listen. For my husband having gone away, no matter how or where, what is it thy intention to do now? Here am I a prey to thee, and utterly defenceless; and now there is absolutely nothing to prevent thee from completing thy design. Tell me, then, what thou art proposing to do. And she waited, while I answered her absolutely nothing, watching her with intoxication, and lurking as it were under the protection of her blindness. And presently she said again: Why art thou silent? Art thou meditating in what manner to appropriate me? Save thyself the trouble, for I myself will tell thee of my own accord. Art thou not a king, with agents about thee for any base design? Send them secretly at night, and steal me, and thy business is done. And she laughed again, and said: Or didst thou think me one, like others, doubtless, such as

thou hast known, to be flattered by the vanity of having a lover in the king? Then why didst thou endeavour to hide from me thy rank? Surely thou wast deserted by thy reason. Art thou not aware, that women, as a rule, flutter round a king like silly moths about a torch, ready to burn up, not only the wings of their reputation, but even their very souls in the form of the honour of their husbands, so that only they may bathe for a moment in his glitter, before shrivelling in its flame? Or didst thou trust in thy favour as a man; for I have heard that no man in thy kingdom can compare with thee: not considering that I was blind, and unable either to admire or dislike thee, even though thy ugliness were such as to frighten me away? Aye, and verily I think, that if thy exterior correspond to what thou art within, thou art surely very ugly; and I rejoice, for the first time in my life, I cannot see. And again she laughed, like one in a fever of desperation, while all the while I stood before her silent, wroth with her and with myself, yet attracted to her rather than repelled, by everything she said.

And all at once she said: Say, Maharáj, what was thy object in originally pursuing me? Come, tell me frankly. Is it not my love that thou wouldst have? And I exclaimed: Aye! it is thy love indeed; and for it I would cast my kingdom into the very bottom of a well. Then she said: See, now, every way thou hast acted like a fool. What! gain a woman's love by murdering her husband! Then what a monster must have been the woman thou art ready to adore! And I said hastily: I am no murderer of thy husband, as I told thee. And

moreover, O thou angry beauty, not every woman loves her husband; and thine is far too old for thee, and leaves thee, moreover, deserted and alone. And instantly, she put up her two hands to stop her ears, exclaiming: Say not a word against my husband, or I will become deaf as well as blind. Why didst thou not rather endeavour to persuade me, he had deserted me in favour of thyself? For had I only been the woman thou art taking me to be, nothing could have been better to the point. Or why didst thou not try to buy me from him? Thou art rich. Was it that it was only too well known to thee, he would not sell me, even for a very mountain of pure gold? Then what art thou but a thief, seeking underhand to rob him of the thing he would not sell?

And Trishodadhi, as he listened, murmured to himself: Aha! well said, well done! O irrefutable wife, well might he stand before thee, in silence and abashed. And oblivious of his muttering, he listened to the tale.

CHAPTER XI

ND the elephant said: O pippala, little as she knew it, she was but pleading against herself, and losing her own cause, even in the winning of it, by making herself ever more and more the mistress of my soul. And all the while she was reducing me as it were to ashes, by the fire of her scorn; strange! she was but raising out of those very

ashes other and far fiercer fire than hers, so unutterably beautiful
was the body and the soul of my despiser. And then all at once, as
if driven to despair by the consciousness of her own forlorn
position, she burst from laughter into tears. And she wept,
rocking herself to and fro before me as she sat, while I watched
her with a heart that almost broke, in despair that I should grieve
her, yet fiercely determined to win her for my own. Ha! very
terrible is the cruelty of love, piercing with marble heart the very
thing it loves with swords; and very wonderful the conduct of a
lover, treating as if with hatred, and pitilessly torturing, the thing
for which he longs to give his life. For I would have given my
kingdom, only to take her in my arms and soothe her; and yet my
heart was adamant to her reproaches, intent on nothing but
breaking her determination, and bending her to my will. And so I
stood, waiting till the tempest of her sorrow should abate, and
allow her to bring about herself a change in a situation, with
which I myself was powerless to deal. And at last she raised her
head, and said: O King, thou seest that I am absolutely at thy
mercy. And hast thou then no pity or compassion? Is it my love
that thou aimest at possessing? Then how will it advantage thee to
take by force, what has value only when it is given of its own
accord? Or what can be the value of a body, dead and without a
soul? Wilt thou love a corpse, or will a corpse relove thee? Callest
thou love, such a union with the dead? I tell thee, such love would
turn to hatred in a day.

And I exclaimed: Ah! Watsatarí; say not, say not, thou canst not love me; and speak not of thyself as dead, who art my life, and as it were, the very soul and self of me. Nay, rather is it I, who am altogether dead, without thee. Aye! all these years I have been dead, having only now at last begun to live, since first I climbed upon the wall, to see my life at last, in thee below. Alas! Watsatarí, and dost thou talk of pity or compassion, that hast thyself no grain of either in that heart of thine, that, as I think, is harder than a stone? Or being blind thyself, dost thou imagine all others also blind? And O that I myself were blind indeed, and could not see thee, for as it is, the sight of thee is poison more fell than any 'kálakuta,'[1] since that at least was drinkable, but thy blue bewildering beauty is fatal even at a distance, showing the traveller a mocking picture in the desert, only to whet his thirst, without allowing him to drink at all. Aye! surely thou art an incarnation of illusion, more bitter even than the ocean with its brine; for thou art salt not only to the taste but to the sight. And why, then, didst thou allure me with the mystery and depth of thy still unfathomable eyes, or lull my senses and dash my reason from its rock by the surge of the wave that throbs in the motion of thy tantalising breast, only to drive me from thee by menaces of death? Did the Creator mould thee to such incomparable form, or bestow on every movement of thy body so delicate and characteristically feminine a grace, only for my destruction? Did he fill me with passionate longing for exactly such a perfect model of the soft and seductive

[1] *The poison that Shiwa drank to save the world, which was blue. In this passage, there is an elaborate play on 'beauty' and 'salt,' which are denoted by the same word.*

sweetness of a woman as thyself, only to show me the reality in derision, and say to me as soon as I had found it, Forget it, and go away, and leave it to another. Nay, but I will not go away, and I tell thee, that in vain dost thou endeavour to deprive me of thyself. Rather will I bind thee to myself, making thee a part of me, as is Gauri of Maheshwara, and thou shalt be the complement and the other half of me, and shrine me in thy heart and thee in mine.

And she said: Nay, but it is impossible, for my husband is between; and it is not thou, but he, who is the idol and the dweller in my shrine.

And Trishodadhi, as he listened, said softly to himself: Out, out upon the husband that could doubt her, even in a dream! And oblivious of his muttering, he listened on, for the remainder of the tale.

CHAPTER XII

ND the elephant said: Pippala, when she spoke, I uttered a cry. And I exclaimed: Ha! the husband! O alas! I had forgotten him. Then she said quietly: But I had not. And I cried: O alas! alas! Out, out upon this husband, for he was born only for my ruin and despair. Now, like a cloud of pitchy black, he stands between my soul, and the digit of the moon that I adore. Aye! but for him, I might be hanging like a moonstone bathed in the nectar camphor of its beams. O why did fate suffer him to come between us! why did I not meet thee first, before he ever saw thee? Ha! what would it cost the Creator to obliterate a single husband, and strike him from the roll of entities, making him absolutely nothing and a thing that has never been, thinner than the memory of a forgotten dream? Alas! I am cheated by the Creator and this husband, and coming just too late, I am robbed of the very fruit of this untimely birth. And after all, what is this husband? Is he a husband who goes away and leaves thee, like a flower dropped negligently upon the road, and have I not found thee, made ownerless by his absence, and picked thee up, to wear thee in my hair? Can he be thy owner, of whom it is not even certain that he lives? Aye! doubtless he is dead, and thou hast not any longer the pretext of a husband, to bar thee from my claim. And instantly she said: Then, if he is really dead, it is my duty to follow him through the fire, which, could I only learn his death with certainty, I would do without delay. And I exclaimed: Nay, nay, dare not to dream of fire, for how knowest thou he is dead? Beyond a doubt, he is not dead, but only hidden; and wouldst thou dream of such criminal impiety as to take it on thyself to precede him into the other world. I tell thee, it is thy duty to await him. And she said: Then if he is not dead, I am no widow, but his wife.

And I exclaimed with tears: Alas! dead or alive, he blocks the way, and I am lost. But what then, if he never should return? What if year follows year, and still he chooses to be absent, while

all the time the lotus of thy beauty fades, and envious wrinkles crawl slowly, one by one, to feed like worms on thy soft delicious skin, and occupy the corner beneath thy little ear, turning thy dark tresses white, as if with fear of the shadow of approaching age and death? Am I to stand idly by, like a spectator, and watch the river of my happiness flow by me, in the form of thy decaying charm? And she said in a low voice: Each night and day I will expect him, and when he comes, let it be when it may, he shall never catch me unprepared, but find me waiting, sad by reason of his absence, and joyous like a city hung with banners to receive its lord, at the moment of his return.

And I gazed at her for a little, poised as it were between affection and despair; for as she spoke, the colour rose and stood upon her cheek, and her lip trembled, and her steady eyes seemed to gaze into the distance, seeing not me, but that absent husband: and I knew that as she said, so would she do. And I wrung my hands, and wept for sorrow. And I exclaimed: Ha! it is unjust, and I am the plaything of a destiny that I fastened on myself by sins committed in a former birth, in the form of this dark shadow of a husband, who is present even in his absence, though as it seems, time and space have swallowed him, as the ocean swallows up a little stone, dropped from the feather of a passing swan into the very middle of the sea. And know, O pippala, that it was exactly as I said. For that husband of hers returned no more, but vanished, and neither I nor any other ever saw him more, or knew where he had gone.

And Trishodadhi, as he listened, said within himself; Ha! little does this elephant imagine who it is, that sits and listens to him now. And oblivious of his muttering, he listened on, eager for the remainder of the tale,

CHAPTER XIII

ND the elephant said: Pippala, as I stood before her, like an incarnation of the struggle between adoration and dismay, she spoke and said: O King Ruru, thou seest it is useless. Cease, then, thy pleading and persuasion, and go away; for all that thou canst urge is wasted breath, and thou art like one striving by reiterated throwing to fix a stone in air, which notwithstanding returns in spite of thee invariably to the ground – as does my heart to the memory of its lord.

And I said: Ha! now I see, I have offended the deity of Love, and the Lord of Obstacles is angry. For the one has turned his back on me, and the other has cast before me this mountain of an obstacle, thy husband, throwing even at a distance a blighting shadow in the form of reminiscence, by which I am buried in blackness and hidden from thy heart. O that thy eyes could see me, for then it might be that through them I might effect an entrance; but alas! the door to thee is shut. Or had I only been blind as well as thou, thou never couldst have entered mine. What! is it right of thee to occupy my heart, and yet bar me from thy own? And she said: My heart is full, and poor, and narrow, and far too small for thee, containing as it does room for only one, and not like thine, royal, and a palace, with chambers for innumerable guests.

And I said, with emotion: Ah! Watsatarí, thy words are very sharp, and like a dagger in my heart; and now I see, that every man is punished by himself, being followed to eternity by actions of his own, black dogs, from which in vain he will endeavour to escape. Aye! thou art right, I turned my heart into a caravanserai, to which I welcomed every worthless guest; but now I swear to thee, the very sight of thee has cleansed it like a pure river, which, ousting everything, has left there nothing, but the crystal of itself. Then she said: O King, they say of thee in the bazaar, that thou wast bent like a golden bar from straight to crooked, by the evil behaviour of thy queen. And is it true? And I said, eagerly: Aye! she it was that turned me, as thou sayest, aside, into the jungle of depravity. And instantly she said, quietly: What! then art thou not ashamed? For what art thou doing now, but striving to make me such another as thy queen, whom, according to thyself, thou blamest, as the cause of thy unhappiness? Thou art thyself the judge. And should I listen to thee, thou tellest me beforehand, I should be utterly worthless in thy eyes, and a discredit to myself, and my husband, and my sex. For the three worlds shudder at the spectacle of a woman that is traitor to her lord. Go then away very quickly, and forget that thou hast ever seen my face.

And Trishodadhi, as he listened, exclaimed in ecstasy to himself: Ha! good wife and subtle argument. Now she has slain him, as it

were, with his very own sword. And utterly oblivious of his muttering, he listened eagerly for the remainder of the tale.

CHAPTER XIV

AND the elephant said: Pippala, as I gazed at her, I almost shrank before her tranquil eyes, half believing she could see me, so utterly had she crushed me by her unanswerable words. And yet, the less I could reply, the more intense became my admiration of herself, and the stronger my unwillingness to obey her, and go away and leave her. And as if her beauty was not enough, her very virtue came to reinforce it, making her attraction a hundred times more powerful than ever. O pippala, what is this mystery of love, and who is there who can sound it? For what was I doing, but endeavouring to persuade her? and yet, had she been persuaded, I should actually have grieved at my success; as I actually rejoiced at her refusal, loving her the better, the less she could be persuaded to love me. And I exclaimed, as if in defiance of despair: No matter, O thou incomparable beauty, what I was, for I am changed, and by thee, in the twinkling of an eye. And what does it matter what they say in the bazaar, for the world is but a straw to me, in comparison with thee? See, I cannot live without thee, and I will carry thee away, to a distance from the world, and be to thee infinitely more than a thousand husbands such as thine. For he neglected thee, and left thee to thyself, not valuing his pearl. But I will be thy other self;

see, thou art blind, but I will be thy eyes, and by means of me, thou shalt utterly forget thy want of sight. And if thou wilt, I will take thee clean away, turning my back upon my kingdom and the world, like yonder necklace which I have left for thy sake lying unregarded in the grass, and asking of thee in return nothing but thyself. Dost thou not know, what fate awaits thee here? Canst thou endure to live, deserted by thy husband, who is either dead or gone, the object of the scorn and derision and hard usage of the world, a very target for the arrows of contempt?[1] What then wilt thou resemble but a blue delicious lotus, trampled in the mire of a city street by the foot of every passer-by; a lotus, whose appropriate position is either the pool in the silence of the forest, or the head of a king? But come with me, O lotus, and thou shalt gain at one stroke both the forest and the king. For here am I, a king, and beside us is the forest, stretching like the ocean to the south, whose farther shore no hunter ever sees. And far away within it, I will build thee a marble palace that shall laugh at even Alaká, set like a pearl in the middle of an emerald of gardens, full of pools of golden lotuses, whose roots are nibbled by a multitude of silver swans. And there by day thou shalt wander led by me, or lie and dream, fanned by breezes heavy with the sandal straight from Malaya, on marble slabs cooled by the spray tossed from the crystal tanks by waterfalls whose music shall pour sleep into thy ear, leaving thee wakeful at midnight to listen and tremble as I guide thee along the palace-top at the cry of the wild animals

[1]*The position of the Hindoo widow was very different from that of other widows: her misfortune was counted to her as a crime, and her life a long-drawn-out martyrdom, from which perhaps the fire would be release.*

roaming at a distance in the wood, till at last thou fall to dreaming in my arms, lulled by the slow and melancholy weeping of the moonstones oozing as they swing to and fro slowly in the moonlight, as if keeping time to the silent dance of their own long shadows on the floor. And what will it matter to thee or me what they say in the bazaar, living together like Siddhas in the moon, to whom this babble of busybodies in the cities of this despicable earth sounds like the recollection of the murmur of a far-off ocean in the dream of a half-remembered birth. And all the while I will be thy servant and the eyes of thee, and my voice shall paint to thee pictures of the world that shall surround thee, and be thy one interpreter, till learning its language, thy soul shall even forget to remember it was blind. And I will utterly efface thy recollection of this husband, who is a husband in nothing but the name, since he leaves thee deserted and alone, to be afflicted; and instead of him I will be thy husband, and thy other half and helper, and thy soother and thy lover and the very eyes and soul of thee.

And Trishodadhi, as he listened, said with anxiety to himself: Ha! now this liar of a king is very cunning, and beyond a doubt, many a woman would have found it hard to resist the flattery of his tongue. And oblivious of his muttering, he listened eagerly for the remainder of the tale.

CHAPTER XV

ND the elephant said: Pippala, as I ended, I stepped forward, and I took her, very gently, by the hand. And then, lo! the very moment that I touched it, she started. And she leaped back, like one that has suddenly put his hand into the flame of a fire, with a cry. And as I watched her, she stood for a single instant, like one balanced on the very verge of flying, or sobbing, or falling to the ground, for she swayed on her little feet, and her body shook all over, like a tree whose leaves are stirred by a sudden wind. And her great breast struggled in violent agitation, as if striving to leap from its bodice in sheer fright. And then in a moment, all at once she changed, becoming still, as though she were an image, carved in stone, upon a temple wall. Only her bosom went on heaving like the sea, as if she could not breathe. And after a while she said, very slowly: My blindness makes my battle hard, for I cannot either see my danger coming, or escape it by flying when it comes. And now, well I discern the terrible consequences of sins committed in a former birth, for now I am without resource, resembling one that walks in inky darkness, whose every step may plunge the point of a sword into his heart. And yet that very blindness which puts me in thy power contains the weapon to defeat thee; for within it I am shut from thee as in an impenetrable fortress, around which thou art wandering in vain. For the Creator has not left even the blind without their proper refuge, and has bestowed upon them inner eyes, as if to balance the want of those without; and being deprived by their infirmity of all that world which others see, they fall back upon the world within, composed of memory and meditation, and patience and emotion, and fidelity and hope. And as I listen to thy words, falling on my ear out of the visible I cannot see, tempting me, and seeking as it were to melt my resolution by a fiery rain, I look into my soul, and I see at a distance, in its darkness, a solitary star in the form of my husband, sending me as it were a ray of support and consolation, to keep me from sinking in the waves of the ocean of despair. And now I tell thee, all thy honied words are worthless, and like arrows, they fall back blunted and shattered on the rock on which I lean, in the form of his memory, and beating on my head like particles of snow they do but add to the mound of cold resistance which they aim removing by their ineffectual storm. And though I know not where he is, nor even if he will return, yet when he does he shall find his honour safe, and my soul like a temple shall preserve within its shrine the candle that he lit, whose steady flame not all the winds of flattery and temptation blown from thine or any other mouth shall ever make extinct, or even cause to flicker for an instant, even in a dream. And like Draupadi, or Damayanti, or Sita, or Sawitri, I shall meet my husband, either in this birth or another, so, as that neither he nor I will be ashamed. And well though I know that I am bodily at thy mercy and in thy power, so that coming thyself or sending others, thou canst carry me by violence away, as I think will be the case, yet shall even that avail thee nothing. For the body thou shalt ravish, as I told thee, will be dead, and its soul will be away. For though it is my duty not to quit it, for my husband has left me, as it were, as a deposit in my own hands to be guarded for himself, yet I shall make no effort to conceal it from thee like a coward; it is here for thee to steal. Take, if thou wilt, a thing that can offer no resistance; thou wilt gain absolutely nothing but dishonour for thyself, loving what will not love thee, embracing what will not embrace thee, doomed to remain everlastingly outside, and baulked of that treasure of the heart within, like a robber with an adamantine casket to which he has no key, and which, defying all his efforts to invade it, leaves him with nothing to reward him but his crime. Aye! try, and thou shalt find, that with nothing to defend it, armed only with a memory, the heart of a woman is stronger than all the power of a king. Aye! bring, if thou wilt, the ocean, and the wind, and the darkness to assist thee, and thou shalt find that the little tongue of that flame which is fed on the oil of reminiscence will utterly refuse to be extinguished by them all.

And Trishodadhi, as he listened, murmured softly to himself: Ah! noble wife, ah! Watsatarí, thou hast annihilated this robber of a king. And utterly oblivious of his muttering, he listened, with a heart on fire, for the remainder of the tale.

CHAPTER XVI

AND the elephant said: Ha! pippala, as she ended, I stood confounded, like a picture on a wall, gazing at her in utter oblivion of everything but herself, drunk with amazement and adoration. For as she spoke, she seemed to grow, and become larger than herself; and her words poured like a stream of liquid fire shot from the fountain of her soul, and my own soul seemed as it were to shrink and grow small before her, like a thing shrivelled in a flame. And her strange calm eyes shone till I shuddered as I saw them, and I felt like the demon whom Gauri was about to annihilate for ever, in her form. And I could have fallen down and worshipped her in ecstasy, and yet for very shame I dared not stir. And so I stood a while, as if in stupor, and then very quietly I crept away, and climbing over the wall, returned privately to my palace, like a thief ashamed. And there, throwing myself upon my bed, I lay silent, unconscious of the passage of time, gazing as it were into darkness, and seeing nothing but the image of Watsatarí, standing still before me, and looking at me fixedly, with eyes from which I strove to hide myself in vain.

And all at once, in the middle of the night, I started up shouting: Watsatarí! Watsatarí! And I raved with words devoid of meaning, feeling nothing but passionate desire for herself and her beauty, and hatred of her husband, and loathing for myself. And I exclaimed: Haha! but for this husband, I might have attained to the

fruit of my birth, which has vanished like a dream.

And as it happened, my wita overheard me, for as a rule he never left me, and he was sitting by my sides, watching me, like a bird of evil omen, with his only eye; for he had lost the other by a blow from a boon companion in a drunken brawl. And all at once he said: Maharáj, doubtless thou art troubled in soul by reason of some love affair; and now, sorrow shared with a friend is lightened of more than half its burden. Moreover, it may be I could help thee, for in every such case, a bystander is a better judge. So in my distress, unable to refrain, I told him the whole story. And when I made an end, the wita said: Maharáj, hadst thou kept this to thyself, thou wouldst not have been well advised; as I shall show thee. For thy opinion is, that the husband is thy difficulty, and the obstacle in this affair. And I said: Aye! so he is, beyond a doubt; and an obstacle utterly beyond removal. Then said the wita: Maharáj, thou art mistaken altogether. For the husband in this case is not an obstacle at all, for he has disappeared, as though on purpose to oblige thee and leave thy way open. But that which stands in thy way, exactly as she said herself, is nothing but his memory.[1] For if she could forget him, she would have absolutely nothing to oppose to thee at all. And I exclaimed: Aye! indeed! if she could forget him. Then said that crafty wita: Did I not say that my assistance would avail thee? For there is absolutely no difficulty in this at all. For I have a friend, who has gone to the very farther shore of the 'Ayurweda,'[2] and possesses skill sufficient to raise the very dead to

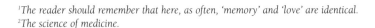

[1] *The reader should remember that here, as often, 'memory' and 'love' are identical.*
[2] *The science of medicine.*

life. And now I will consult him, and tell him only so much as is necessary to the business in hand, and get from him a drug to annihilate the memory; and what can be more easy than for such a very Lord of Herbs[1] to produce oblivion and forgetfulness, by the means of a drug? For if she could only be induced to lose, somehow or other, all recollection of her husband, remaining in every other point the same, thy object is attained, and stealing into her soul, thou couldst very easily fill it with thy image, being vacant of his own.

And instantly I uttered a cry, and falling on my wita, embraced him, intoxicated with delight, exclaiming: Ha! most admirable of all witas, if thou canst actually do as thou hast said, I will weigh myself in gold, for thy reward. And like thy own physician, thou hast as it were raised me from the dead. And now let us begin and set to work, without losing any time. And in my agitation I could hardly endure to wait for the return of day. Then very early in the morning the wita went to his physician and returned, holding in his hands a little phial. And he said: Maharáj, I have the cure for every recollection in this glass. For as he gave it me, he said: Whoever swallows this will fall asleep, to lose on reawakening every vestige of recollection of what happened in his life before. So nothing now remains, except the drinking. And to drink, she must be here. And if thou wilt, I will take assistance, and go and bring her, and put her in thy hands myself. And if thy beauty will not come, what matter? A little violence will do no harm, since all will be forgotten when she wakes.

[1] *A common epithet of the moon.*

And then, he fixed on me his eye, as if ironically, and I shuddered as I saw it, saying to me as it were significantly: Thou and I. And I looked at him with horror, saying to myself: What! shall I share her with this wita, and shall the lotus of her body be defiled by his handling, even in a dream? And I leaped at him and struck him to the ground, exclaiming furiously: Dog of a wita, dost thou dare? Is it for such a thing as thou art to lay hands on her, or shall she be profaned by the grasp of such a monster as thyself?

And Trishodadhi, as he listened, muttered to himself in wrath: Ha! thou that callest others monsters, what of thyself? what defilement was there in the touch of thy filthy wita, that was not doubled by the profanation in thy own? And all oblivious of his muttering, he listened with anxiety for the conclusion of the tale.

CHAPTER XVII

ND the elephant said: Pippala, as the wita rose, I said to him in wrath: I only will go to fetch her, nor shall any finger touch her but my own. And as for thee, remain behind, and await me with thy phial till I come. Then said the wita: As the Maharáj chooses. And he bowed before me like a slave, and listened in silence while I made my preparations, thinking no more of him, and utterly forgetful of the injuries he had suffered at my hands. But if I forgot them, so did not he. Ha! wonderful is the blindness of kings and lovers who, intoxicated with passionate desire, place with open eyes weapons in the hands of infuriated enemies, who only await an opportunity to stab them to the heart.

And then, O pippala, in the evening, I mounted my horse, and went, with a chosen band of confidential servants, and a litter, secretly to the garden. And I rode very slowly, thinking how I should induce her to come away, unwilling to use force. And I said to myself, with hesitation: But if she will not come, as only too much I fear, what then? Must I not have recourse to violence? And after all, was not my wita right? What matter a little violence, to be utterly forgotten as soon as she awakes? Moreover, being blind, how can she tell who seizes her, seeing that she knows me by nothing but my voice? And yet I could not bring myself to think of taking her away by force, striving to discover some other way, and saying to myself: Could I but discover something, to make her come away with me of her own accord.

And then, all at once, I stopped short. And I exclaimed: Ha! I have it. Surely this will bring her; and now, the business is done.

And I set spurs to my horse, and followed by my train, I quickly reached the garden, and leaving them to wait below, I climbed the wall alone, and looked, and lo! there she stood again, listening, and looking as it were towards me, exactly as she did at first.

And then, strange! the instant that I saw her, I stopped, looking down at her upon the wall, and such a sadness mingled with the ecstasy of my devotion as I watched her, that the tears rose up into my eyes. And I said

to myself: Let me look at her well, for just a little while, for this is the very last time I shall see her from the wall. Ha! pippala, little did I dream that I was looking at her, never again to see her standing, either from the wall or any other place whatever in the world. And her dress, as she had turned round towards the wall, startled by the sound of my approach, was twined as if with affection, like a creeper, closely round her ankles, and had wrapped itself around her feet, as if to hinder them from moving and root her in the ground, resembling a pedestal, out of which, like a statue of herself, her beautiful undulating body rose up into the air, like the feminine incarnation of a full-blown and heavy flower, only waiting for a breeze to sway gently on its slender stalk. And once more I trembled as I gazed at the dead still colour of her tranquil unintimidated eyes, that seemed as it were to say to me, Coward, couldst thou have mustered courage to lay rude hands on such a lovely lotus as myself, growing in a pool which is not thine?

And suddenly, I flung myself into the garden, and went hastily towards her. And I exclaimed: Watsatarí, thy husband is returned, for I have found him, and now I have him in my palace, and his life is in my hands, and thine. And now I have come myself, with an escort, to bring thee to him; so that in thy presence I may bargain with him for thee, and buy thee, at any price that he shall name. Didst thou not say, I was a robber, endeavouring to steal the thing I could not buy? And now, then, we shall see whether he will sell thee; and I promise thee, I will not buy thee cheap; for I am ready to give him, in return for thee, his life.

And as she listened, she started; and when I ended, she was silent; and as I watched her, she trembled a very little, and grew pale. And presently she said slowly: Thou hast placed me, indeed, in an extremity; and very sore indeed is my perplexity, to know what I should do. And what if I refuse to come? And I said in a low voice: It will go hard with thy husband, in thy absence. Ah! pippala, I pitied her, even as I spoke. And I steeled myself against compassion, saying to myself: No matter if she suffers a little now; for very soon, I will make it up to her, a thousandfold and more.

And after a while, she sighed and said again: How can I believe thee, who hast lied to me so often, and whose purpose only too well I understand? Yet how can I resist one who can so easily effect by violence the end at which he aims, if I refuse? And yet, I fear for my husband, and what thou sayest may, after all, be true. Wilt thou swear to me, thou wilt take me to my husband? And I said to myself: She has caught herself in the trap; and who will be her husband but myself? And I exclaimed: Watsatarí, if I am lying to thee, may I fall into a lower birth! Ha! pippala, as I think, the deity was listening, and bound me in this very body of an elephant, remembering my words, in obedience to my own curse.

And Trishodadhi, as he listened, murmured to himself: Ah! liar of a king, so after all, thou couldst prevail on her virtue only by making use of me against myself, and turning as it were her very heart into a snare. And all oblivious of his muttering, he listened eagerly for the termination of the tale.

CHAPTER XVIII

AND the elephant said: Pippala, she yielded at the last. And she said, in a low voice: May my husband forgive me, if my better judgment is in error, overlooking my own danger for his sake. But it will be necessary to carry me, for, as I think, my body will not move of its own accord. And then, all at once, she reeled, and would have fallen, swooning at my feet, but that I sprang forward, and caught her as she fell. And very carefully I lifted her in my arms, bereft as she was of sense, and in my intoxication, unable to refrain, I kissed her as she lay unconscious in my arms, and lo! she was as cold as ice. And I called to my assistants, and got her with their help over that wall, that resembled the last obstacle in the road of my delight, and placing her in the litter, I carried her away very quickly to my palace, riding beside her with a soul that danced as it were with joy and agitation, while all the while she lay as if her own soul abandoning its body had stayed behind her in the garden, refusing to be a traitor to its trust. And as soon as we arrived, once more I took her in my arms, and carried her within, and placed her, just as she was, upon a couch. And I said to my wita, who was waiting: Bring now very quickly fans, and snow and sandal, and camphor and aromatics, and let us bring her to herself. And so, as I was fanning her, and sprinkling her with icy scents, all at once, she stirred. And she put out her hand, as if groping to feel who was beside her, and she murmured, Water, water! so low as hardly to be heard.

And at that very moment, I looked, and saw the wita, gazing at me with his eye. And he whispered: Maharáj, shall I give it? And I said: Give it me, and I will give it her myself. And I took the water from his hands, and emptied into it the phial; and I put the water to her lips, and very greedily she drank. Ah! woe is me, I gave it, and she drank. Ha! very wonderful is the terrible mystery of the consequence of works, bound in whose adamantine chain we move, and blunder, not seeing where we go, not knowing what we do, bringing about with open eyes the very opposite of the end at which we aim. Ah! I, who would have abandoned not one, but an infinity of bodies, only to save her from a scratch, only to keep a single hair from falling from her head, I, with these hands, I gave her that water, and she drank, while all the while the wita stood watching, like destiny in human form, incarnate in a body that was destitute of any heart.

And Trishodadhi, as he listened, murmured to himself: Ha! better it were to have no heart at all, than such a heart as thine. And all oblivious of his muttering, he listened to the tale.

CHAPTER XIX

ND the elephant said: Pippala, she drank, and instantly fell back upon the couch, and lay, paler than the digit of the moon by day, and still as a picture painted on a wall. And I said in exultation and triumph to myself: Now, leave her and let it work, and in the meantime, I will watch her till she wakes. And now, all her suffering and trial is over; and little indeed shall she have cause to complain of changing that old husband for myself. And I said to my wita: Now, begone, and leave me alone with her; and to-morrow I will see to thy reward. And as he went, that wita whispered in my ear: Maharáj, the business is done. Now then, very soon, she will have utterly forgotten all, and thy turn to play the husband has arrived. And he gazed at me for a moment with a smile of evil omen, and I was troubled as I saw it, for his eye resembled that of a vulture sitting on a cemetery wall. Alas! even then, I did not understand. And then he went away, vanishing like Trishodadhi in the ocean of the world. Ha! wise he was to disappear, for well he knew that on the morrow, the very sight of me would have been the signal of his death.

And when he had gone, I remained alone in that chamber with Watsatarí, to watch till she awoke. And I wandered up and down, as it were on tiptoe, with agitated steps, while the night crept slowly on, hour after hour, and every now and then I stopped to look at her as she lay upon the couch; and like a wild beast in a cage, I went to and fro, unable to remain at rest, tossed here and there by the tumult in my soul, where anticipation and impatience, and desire and triumph and delight, and doubt and apprehension jostled each other like waves of the sea, roused into disquiet by the wind of passion, and yet pervaded by unutterable longing to grow calm and be still at the sight of that lovely digit of the moon rising as it were to quell it in an instant and allay its storm, by awaking from her sleep. And in the meantime, the light of the real moon grew gradually stronger, and stole into the room, as if desirous to become reunited with that sleeping beauty that resembled a portion of himself.[1] And seeing it, I said within myself: Surely the moon is right, and now he shall have his wish; for I am not jealous of sharing her with such a lover. And I extinguished all the lamps, and threw open all the trellises, and I sat down on a couch a little way off, and watched her beauty and adored it as she lay, bathed in the soft and silver light of that lord of heavenly nectar. And the shadows of the strings of the moonstones hanging in rows along the windows fell over her in stripes that resembled the bars of a cage, as if wishing to keep her prisoner against her will. And so as I watched her in ecstasy, the sound of the camphor ooze dropping slowly every now and then on the marble floor below murmured in my ear like music and a melody of slumber, and played on the fatigue and agitation of my soul, and at last, all unawares, I fell asleep.

[1] *The moon proper is a male; but all his digits are feminine.*

And all at once, I awoke, and started up, and looked, and lo! the moonlight had all but gone. And in the darkness, lit as it were by the shadow of his last remaining ray, which fell upon her, I saw her lying, absolutely still, exactly as she lay before. And suddenly, as I saw her, I began to tremble like a leaf. And in the silence, I heard my own heart beating, as if it wished to wake her, like the noise of a drum. And all my hair suddenly stood on end, and the sweat broke out upon my brow. And I said to myself: Ha! she is very still, lying exactly as she lay before, never having moved.

And I stood gazing at her in a stupor, and listening to my own heart, that beat in my ears like the surge of the sea. And then, very slowly, I went silently on tiptoe up to that couch on which she lay. And I bent over her, listening, and all at once I touched her with my hand. Ha! pippala, she was colder than the marble floor. And she smiled in that dying moonlight, saying as it were: Maharáj I was right after all; and as I told thee, thou hast stolen my body, only to find it deserted by the soul.

THE WAVES OF TIME

And many lave their souls in the wave,

For brine is a sort of breath,

And death is a kind of life resigned,

As this life is a death.

Danda

THE WAVES OF TIME

AND then, as he listened, all at once that old Brahman Trishodadhi rose to his feet. And as he did so, he looked towards the elephant, and lo! like a flash of lightning, that elephant suddenly disappeared. And in his place he saw no elephant, but King Ruru, standing still, exactly as he lived before. And no sooner had he seen him, than King Ruru exclaimed in delight: Ha! now my story is concluded, and now the curse is ended, and I have escaped from that terrible body of an elephant, to regain my own proper form of a man.

And as Trishodadhi looked towards him, almost abandoning the body, for wonder at the thing he saw, all at once his eyes almost started from his head, and every hair upon his body stood erect. For there, close beside the tree stood Watsatarí herself, exactly as that elephant Ruru had described her, with her head a little bent, like one that listens, and her great eyes turned, exactly as of old, full upon Trishodadhi himself. And at that very moment, King Ruru shouted in amazement and in intoxication: Watsatarí! What! Watsatarí! What! have I regained thee also, in addition to my life?

And as he listened, all at once the heart of that old Brahman bounded in his body like a deer. And every vestige of his purpose and his muttering vanished from his soul like a dream. And he ran with feet that resembled wings straight towards them, crying aloud in agony and despair, not knowing what he said: Ah! she is mine.

Ah! robber of a king, she is not thine. Ah! she is mine. And he reached them, and ran between them, and threw himself upon Watsatarí, and caught her in his arms, and kissed her, weeping in an ecstasy of grief and repentance and delight, exclaiming as he did so: Ah! dearer than my life; ah! Watsatarí; ah! noble wife, forgive me, for I did not know.

And then, strange! as she threw around his neck soft clinging arms, returning his kisses with her own, there came from her lips a peal of laughter, that rang in his very face. And as he drew back in amazement, he looked, and lo! he was holding in his arms not Watsatarí, but another woman, absolutely strange to him, who gazed upon him as she laughed with derision in her eyes. And she exclaimed: Ha! Trishodadhi, I am not blind, but I see thee very well. And now it is not easy to decide, between thy wife and thyself, which is the better lover. For as it seems it was not she, so much as thou, that needed a little of that medicine of oblivion, to enable thee to play the part of an ascetic, to whom women are as nothing in comparison with austerity and penance. Surely thy love for Watsatarí was wonderful, for thou hast utterly forgotten all thy muttering, and bartered all the mountain of thy merit for a kiss. Yet this much I will tell thee, to console thee, that it is not a nymph of heaven to whom thou hast succumbed.

And then with a laugh she disappeared. And as Trishodadhi stood, struck with the thunderbolt of stupefaction, he looked, and lo! Ruru also vanished, and instead of him, Indra stood before him in the guise of a devotee. And he looked with cold eyes upon Trishodadhi, and said very slowly: O Trishodadhi, the wise strive for wisdom, and gain at least humility. But thine was a false devotion, and could not stand the test. And now, as she said, the mountain of thy merit is utterly annihilated, consumed in a single instant of impure desire like a blade of dry grass in a forest conflagration. And as experiment has proved, regret for the things of sense was not extinct in thee, and the sparks of vanity and egoism and delusion in the form of women lay lurking in the ashes of thy soul, needing only a little breeze of recollection to fan them into flame. And now thou hast allowed the sorrow for the loss of old mundane ties of long ago to conquer thy desire of emancipation and break in upon thy devotion to thy vow. And thou hast been guilty of sinister designs against heaven, springing not from the seed of true and singlehearted resignation, but selfishness and wounded vanity and malice. Fall therefore as a punishment instantly into the body of a dog without a tail. And after that thou shalt become an ape, and then a worm, and afterwards a ravenous flesh-eating Rákshasa, and a jackal, and a domba, and a leatherworker, and a chandàla, and a woman, and many other such garments of a guilty soul, and like a drop of water thou shalt run through an interminable series of miserable births, never discerning any end. For this action of thine has dyed thy soul with so indelible a stain, that the ocean could more easily divest itself of colour and of brine, than thy soul will find it to regain its crystal purity, by cleansing its essence of such an inky blot.

And then, like a flash of lightning, that culprit of a Brahman disappeared.

So then, as the Moony-Crested deity made an end, instantly the Daughter of the Snowy Mountain asked him: O Wearer of the Moon, was then the story told by Indra as an elephant to that crafty Kalánidhi as a tree, a true story, or a figment devised between them to delude him?

And Maheshwara answered: O Snowy One, it was absolutely true, in every item and particular and detail. For Indra came to me, and I told him all about it, showing it to him, exactly as it happened, in the mirror of the past. And even its upshot might have taught thee, that the story was true. For he who listens to a recital of a past, of which he was himself a part, resembles a swan, swift to separate the milk of reality from the water of invention, and the very slightest deviation on the part of the narrator, giving rise to a suspicion, and jarring on the ear like a false note in a harmony, would have burst the illusion like a bubble. For there is no form of persuasion or deception so potent as the simple truth.

Then said Párwati again: Then am I very sorry for that poor old Brahman, who was much to be pitied.

And the Lord of the Moony Tire said: Nay, O Daughter of the Snow, thou art in error. Waste not thy pity on one who deserves absolutely none. For had he really loved Watsatarí his wife, who well deserved it, he would never have gone away and left her, condemning her without appeal, unheard, relying on nothing but the very fallacious testimony of his eyes. For there is no degree of evidence, whether of eyes, or of ears, or of any other sense, which true love would not utterly refuse to credit or receive, against that conviction begotten by love, confiding in its object, seeing that love is absolutely free from any shadow of suspicion, and clings to its faith in spite and in the teeth of all. But jealousy belongs only to a spurious love that is really only vanity and egoism in disguise, and is therefore never sure, but everlastingly uneasy, like Trishodadhi. And as his love was founded on selfishness and vanity, so was also the ambition that replaced it, and they both failed miserably when subjected to the test. And being thus unable either to trust in his wife, or forget her, he deserves nothing but contempt, and came to that miserable end which destiny prepares for all who dishonour the sublime by fraudulent and feeble imitation or pretence. For pure love resembles yonder rock, that refuses to be shaken by any wind whatever, and pure renunciation resembles yonder bird, that floats in the inaccessible serenity of heaven far above, not for parade, but simply because it is its very nature to soar into the blue.

And now, as I said, here is Kailàs, and this is the termination of the tale.

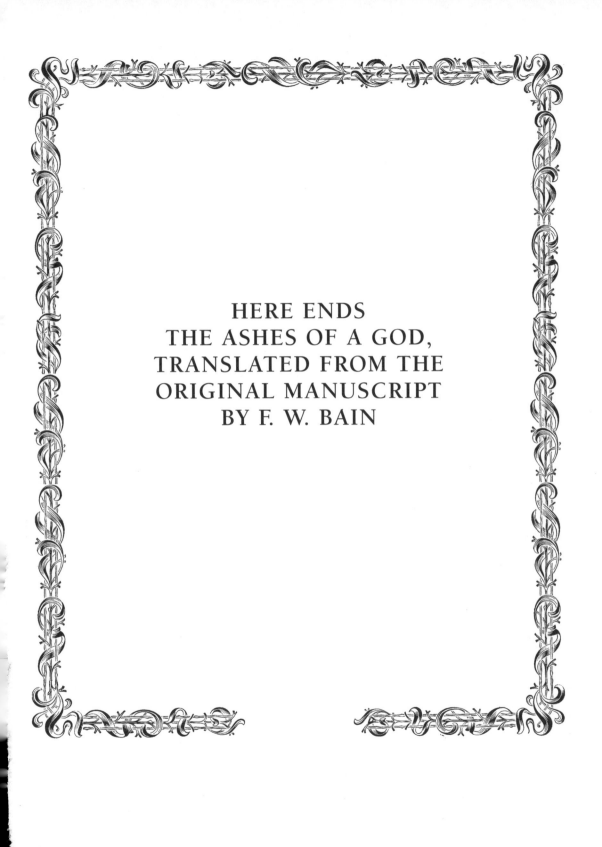

HERE ENDS
THE ASHES OF A GOD,
TRANSLATED FROM THE
ORIGINAL MANUSCRIPT
BY F. W. BAIN